Senior Civil S and Information Technology: Experience of a Pilot Management Development Programme

Evelyn Blennerhassett

Institute of Public Administration

First published 1987
by the Institute of Public Administration
57–61 Lansdowne Road, Dublin 4

ISBN 0 906980 74 7 paperback

Work Motivation and Personnel Practices, a Study of Civil Service Executive Staff, by Evelyn Blennerhassett was published by the Institute of Public Administration in 1983 and **Absenteeism in the Public Service: Information Systems and Control Strategies**, with Patricia Gorman, in 1986.

Printed in Ireland by Criterion Press Limited, Dublin

CONTENTS

ACKNOWLEDGMENTS

This study was commissioned and financed by the former Department of the Public Service (DPS). The Institute of Public Administration wishes to acknowledge the contribution of the Department to the research.

In undertaking the research, I was fortunate to have the advice and support of an excellent project advisory committee. I am particularly grateful to Gerry Colgan (Central Computing Services), Chairman of the Project Advisory Committee, for the personal encouragement and practical help he gave throughout the project, and to Pat Hall, Head of Research in the IPA for valuable guidance and support.

I extend my thanks to the members of the Project Advisory Committee: Seamus Clince, Information Management Advisory Service (IMAS), Paddy Doyle (Consultant), Mary Rose Greville (IPA), John Haskins (CCS), Cyril Havelin (Department of Social Welfare), Ross Hinds (An Post), Tom Murray (Civil Service Training Centre), Rory O'Shea (Department of Social Welfare), Tim Thurston (Guinness Ireland, Ltd.) and Matt Whelan (Department of Health).

Martin Ruddock, my co-worker during Phase 1 of the research, prepared the material on which Appendices C, D and E are based. His contribution is gratefully acknowledged.

Particular thanks are due to Vera Dervan (Department of Social Welfare) for her unstinting support, patience and efficiency during Phase 2. Her contribution to the

management development programme in the Department of
Social Welfare was a major one.

It was a pleasure to work with the members of the
Management Information Technology (MIT) Group:
Brendan Dillon, Joe Doyle, Sean Halpin, Cyril Havelin,
Bill Kelleher, Benny Kevitt, Pat Kirby, Joe Madden,
Justin McCarthy, Dave Power and Paul Wilson.

I would also like to thank Jim Duffy (IMAS), John Haskins
(CCS) and Mick Battle (Social Welfare) for their valuable
contributions to the MIT group programme.

Within the Institute, Breeda Doyle, Deborah Adams and
Caroline Byrne provided excellent administrative support
and typing services. Jonathan Williams' expert help in
preparing the report for publication is also gratefully
acknowledged.

Evelyn Blennerhassett
Research Division

CHAPTER 1

INTRODUCTION

1.1 Focus of Report

This report on senior civil servants and information
technology in Ireland was commissioned through the
Committee for Administrative Research. It discusses
the areas of technology-related skill and knowledge
likely to be needed by senior managers in future
years and, based on the experience of a pilot
development programme in a selected government
department, explores the feasibility and effectiveness
of an in-house, group learning strategy in fostering
these skills and knowledge.

1.2 Research Background

Interest in the <u>organisational</u> effects of new
technology is a relatively recent phenomenon in
Ireland. Most research has concentrated on the
<u>employment</u> effects of technology, i.e., the extent to
which it affects or is likely to affect the number of
jobs in particular employment categories.
Comparatively little attention has been paid to its
likely impact on internal organisational practices and
structures, e.g., its effect on job content and
design, decision-making and control systems, individual

responsibilities, skills, training needs and career patterns. Such research as has been undertaken on these internal organisational issues has tended to focus on the way technonogy affects the jobs of staff at the lowest levels of the hierarchy - in particular, the ergonomic and health aspects associated with working at a visual display unit (VDU). Such a narrow focus was understandable in the 1970s when almost all computer applications were of the routine data processing type, confined to a relatively small area of organisational activity and affecting only a small number of staff, principally at the clerical or "production" level.

Yet the effect of such computer systems on the day-to-day work of senior and middle management tended to be marginal. In most instances, there was little visible evidence of technology, the scale of computerisation being too small to justify the employment of specialist computer staff or the installation of separate computer facilities. The services of external computer bureaux were used to develop, operate and maintain such computerised systems as the organisation possessed. The actual working environment was changed very little and the level of awareness of technology remained generally low.

Such was the situation until comparatively recently in both the private and public sectors. In the civil service, for example, most government departments and agencies relied heavily on the services of the Central Data Processing Services (CDPS). The Office of the Revenue Commissioners and the former Department of Posts and Telegraphs were the two exceptions. Both these organisations were early entrants into the computer field and had built up substantial independent computer facilities and expertise before the establishment of the CDPS in 1973.

However, the position has changed rapidly since the late 1970s, with the advent of relatively cheap but powerful mini- and micro-computers, advances in telecommunications technology and the increased availability of "off-the-shelf" software packages. In many instances, technological and cost considerations now favour the decentralised computer facility and increasing numbers of organisations are installing their own mini- and micro-computers. Applications that would not have been considered even five years ago are now cost-justified and relatively easy to install. This trend towards the development of local computing facilities is also evident in the civil service where, to an increasing extent, mini- and micro-computer-based systems are being installed in line departments, such as the Department of Social Welfare, the Land Registry and Dublin's Metropolitan Courts.

In the Irish civil service, as elsewhere, this trend towards decentralisation of computer facilities has raised the important issue of responsibility and accountability. A major review of government computing services was undertaken in 1982/84 which resulted in a number of significant organisational and structural changes being made. In February 1985, Central Data Processing Services was reorganised into three separate bodies: (i) Central Computing Service (CCS) which provides a bureau service to departments and offices which do not have their own computer facilities and develops and maintains common or civil

service-wide applications such as payroll; (ii)
Information Management Advisory Service (IMAS) which
formulates policy, coordinates computer developments
in the civil service as a whole, and offers a
consultancy service to government departments; and
(iii) Control Section which assesses the
computerisation plans of departments and sanctions
expenditure on computerisation projects. These
organisational changes have been accompanied by a
significant shift in roles and responsibilities:
line departments may draw upon the advice and
expertise of CCS, IMAS and the Control Section, but
responsibility for the formulation of technology
plans and the control and management of computer
systems has been formally devolved to senior
management in each government department.

Decentralisation is likely to increase local
management's awareness of the extent to which their
department has become or is becoming critically
dependent on computerised systems for its day-to-day
administration. The necessity and importance of
ensuring local control and responsibility over
developments in the computer field will become
increasingly more important. As a result, it will no
longer be possible to leave the planning and
development of computer services in the hands of
computer specialists, especially in those instances
where specialist staff are hired from outside the
department. Managers at all levels in the civil
service will be required to assume responsibility for
the administration and control of computerised systems.
They will have to manage the "information resource"
with as much care and attention as they have
traditionally given to the surveillance of other

departmental resources, such as finance and personnel.

A second important consequence of the trend towards
the decentralisation of computer hardware is that it
is likely to lead to a greater awareness of the
potential uses of computers generally, even in
departments that could not be considered to be
technologically advanced. Although most existing
computer-based systems in the Irish civil service
are of the routine data processing type, computers
are being used increasingly in other areas, e.g.,
office administration (principally word processing)
and as an aid to management decision-making,
financial planning, budgeting and forecasting. The
"computer era" of the 1960s and 1970s has given way
to the "information era" of the 1980s, when the
emphasis is on the quality of information produced
rather than on the quantity of reduced clerical
paperwork.[1] As the concept of the computer as a
management tool (rather than as a "beast of burden",
doing routine work) becomes more widespread in the
civil service and the numbers of mini- and microcomputers proliferate, it is reasonable to assume that
the demand for management information/enquiry/analysis
systems will increase. Again, decentralisation will
facilitate other types of applications, principally
in office automation. These newer types of computer
applications tend to make greater use of advanced
technologies such as interactive on-line systems,
data base, high-level user languages, computer models,
telecommunications networking, and so on, than do
traditional record-keeping or transaction-based

[1] W.R. Synnott and W.H. Gruber, Information Resource
    Management: Opportunities and Strategies for
    the 1980s. New York: John Wiley & Sons, Inc.,
    1981, p.5.

systems. They also require more active participation
and supervision by the user than do routine data
processing systems.[1]

To make the best use of these new information
technologies, managers in the civil service will
require different knowledge and skills, both to
control and manage individual computer projects and to
contribute to the development of departmental plans for
information technology generally. Without such
expertise, a department's approach to computerisation
is likely to be piecemeal and the probability of such
dangers occurring as serious system breakdowns,
industrial relations problems, fraud and incompatible
equipment becomes that much greater. Managers will
require considerable assistance and training to
enable them undertake the tasks and responsibilities
posed by information technology. Training and
development programmes are clearly needed. It is
hoped that this research report will contribute
towards meeting this need by outlining a possible form
and content for such a programme.

1.3   Research Objective and Research Strategy

The objective of the research is:

> To devise a management development programme
> for user management in government departments
> and agencies, which would help managers
> assume responsibility for the development and
> operation of computerised information
> processing systems in these departments and
> agencies.

---

[1]   Synnott and Gruber, op. cit. p.6.

In essence, this objective seeks to answer two
separate, though inter-related questions:

What do user managers need to know in order to
be able to plan and manage computerised systems
effectively?

How might managers be helped to acquire this
knowledge and skill?

Although content (what?) issues inevitably overlap
with questions of process (how?), the distinction is,
nevertheless, useful in that it focuses attention on
aspects of the problem that otherwise might not be
addressed directly.

The research was undertaken in two phases. Phase 1
sought to identify the core subject areas which ought
to be included in a technology-orientated development
programme for senior managers in the civil service and
to specify how such a programme might be organised and
implemented. Phase 2 was action-orientated and
involved the mounting of a pilot programme in a
government department to evaluate the feasibility and
effectiveness of the approach proposed in Phase 1.

The research strategy was guided more by practical
considerations than by theoretical concerns. This
conformed with a wish that the research orientation
should be as practically relevant as possible,
resulting in pragmatic recommendations and
guidelines and contributing towards a better
understanding of the issues and problems involved in
implementing a technology-orientated management
development programme in the Irish civil service.

1.4 Report Content

Chapter 2 outlines the initial (Phase 1) proposal for
a technology-orientated management development
programme in terms of objectives, basic content and
format, and describes the approach adopted in
reaching this proposal. Chapter 3 focuses on the
implementation and outcomes of a pilot experimental
development programme modelled on the Phase 1
proposal. Chapter 4 reflects upon the experience
and insights gained from the pilot programme and makes
a number of specific recommendations for improving
technology-orientated management development in the
Irish civil service.

CHAPTER 2

TOWARDS A PROPOSAL FOR A TECHNOLOGY-ORIENTATED
MANAGEMENT DEVELOPMENT PROGRAMME

2.1 First Steps

Three areas are of particular concern in the initial
design stages of any management development programme:

- defining the objectives of the programme

- identifying the learning needs of participants
   and specifying the subject areas which ought to
   be addressed in the programme

- specifying how the programme might be organised
   and implemented.

During Phase 1 of the research, these three areas were
explored in detail by:

- interviewing line managers at Assistant Principal
   and Principal Officer level in a number of
   government departments and agencies. All were
   managers who were currently endeavouring to cope
   with the problems and so take advantage of the
   opportunities that accompany the transition from
   manual to computerised systems of work

- holding a research workshop on the topic of
   "Senior Civil Servants and Information
   Technology: Pathways to the Future", at which
   experienced line managers, computer specialists

and management analysts discussed the subjects
that ought to be included in a management
development programme

- reviewing the syllabi of training programmes for
  user managers of public service and commercial
  training organisations in Ireland and the United
  Kingdom (e.g., IPA, Irish Management Institute,
  Civil Service College, National Computing Centre)

- reviewing the literature on management
  development/training practices, identifying
  current trends and theories

- discussing the feasibility and desirability of
  various management development strategies with
  experienced training specialists in Ireland.

In addition, a survey of current and planned computer
applications in the Irish civil service was carried
out and the researchers visited Britain and Sweden
to see how civil service administrations there
approached the question of user management training.
These visits proved disappointing: neither country
had a planned technology-orientated management
development programme on the lines envisaged in the
present study.

The objectives, content and implementation strategy
proposed at the end of Phase 1 are outlined in the
following sections. The extent to which these
proposals proved feasible and useful in practice is
discussed in Chapter 3.

2.2 Defining the Objectives of the Proposed Development
Programme

The broad objectives of the proposed development
programme were clarified early in the research process
through discussions with potential participants and
senior managers with responsibility for both
computerisation and training in the Irish civil
service.

It was decided that the aim of the programme should
not be to make managers into computer experts. Rather
was the programme seen as a means of promoting more
extensive and active involvement by managers in the
sphere of information technology by:

- increasing their knowledge and understanding of
  information technology in general

- increasing their knowledge and understanding of
  the applicability and potential of technology
  to their department and specific areas of
  responsibility

- alerting them to the problems and opportunities
  associated with the use of technology, in
  particular, to the need for information systems
  planning

- improving their practical skills in specific
  areas e.g., project management and control
  techniques, security aspects of computer systems,
  the use of microcomputers.

It was agreed that the programme should prepare managers
for probable future roles, as well as help them to

become more effective in their present roles. The
development of an informed and committed senior
management cadre in government departments and
agencies was seen as a very important outcome of the
proposed technology-orientated training. Accordingly,
it was decided that the programme should emphasise
greater organisational effectiveness as much as
greater individual effectiveness.

2.3 Identifying Managers' Technology-related Learning Needs

To be relevant and useful, the content of any
management development programme must be based on a
thorough analysis of participants' learning needs. The
identification of these needs is a relatively easy
task when the tasks and responsibilities of
participants are known or can be determined. Such was
not the case in the present research. In the Irish
civil service, as elsewhere, experience and knowledge
of how senior managers' roles and responsibilities are
changing (or are likely to change), as information
technology becomes more important and dominant in
organisations, is very limited. The little we know
is derived almost exclusively from case studies of
single organisations and futurist "scenario-painting"
articles and reports. This lack of practical
experience and understanding posed particular problems
for the research since a programme was being devised
to prepare managers for tasks and responsibilities
that were largely undetermined. In identifying how
information technology is likely to affect managers
in the Irish civil service, therefore, we had to rely
primarily on the views of computer experts, management
analysts, training specialists and a small number of

line managers with personal experience of technological change. These sources indicated that, in future years, the roles of line managers in the civil service will most likely expand to encompass the following technology-related tasks and responsibilities:

Future Technology-related Responsibilities of Managers

- identifying the information processing needs of his or her section or division

- identifying, with the help of specialist support staff, possible solutions (both technological and non-technological) to information processing problems

- investigating the advantages and disadvantages of particular hardware/software options (e.g., by visiting organisations that have some experience of using a particular software package or piece of hardware)

- monitoring and controlling the development and implementation of computer systems

- ensuring that the installed system meets the requirements of the section or division

- ensuring that the system is secure and that confidential data are kept private

- justifying expenditures on information technology

- arranging for staff training

- generating support and commitment from staff

- ensuring that the changeover from manual to computerised systems takes place smoothly

- examining the effects of computer systems on working conditions and the tasks of various levels of staff

- making changes, as appropriate, to structures, procedures and practices

- monitoring and auditing systems after they have been installed to ensure that the expected benefits are realised

- identifying ways in which technology can improve organisational efficiency and effectiveness

- contributing to the development of departmental plans for information technology.

The principle underlying all of the above responsibilities is that of devolving responsibility for computer-based systems to the appropriate level – the individual manager or the individual department. This process of devolution and delegation is already underway in some government departments; it is expected to accelerate in future years as the civil service becomes more technologically advanced.

2.4 Identifying the Main Subject Areas to be Addressed in the Proposed Programme

Government departments differ greatly in the extent to which they use computer technology. Some are already major users (e.g., the Office of the Revenue Commissioners, the Department of Social Welfare); others are at a comparatively early stage of technological development (e.g., the Departments of Energy and the Environment). Each department will continue to follow different technological paths.

These differences must be reflected in the type and content of technology-orientated training offered to managers. For this reason, we did not attempt to devise a "once-and-for-all" development programme for the entire civil service. Instead, the emphasis was on identifying broad subject areas which were likely to be of relevance to most managers in most government departments - a "menu" of topics which would help departments devise training programmes to meet their particular developmental needs.

As a first step in the identification of these core topics, groups of managers at assistant principal and principal officer level were asked to consider their learning needs in relation to technology. Both in group discussion and in personal interviews, their perceptions of what they needed to know about information technology were generally quite modest. For most interviewees, the term "computerisation" was synonymous with traditional data processing (DP) - a fast, efficient means of processing large volumes of routine information, such as social welfare claims. Few had any experience of the "new technology", i.e., the use of computers in non-DP areas, such as management decision-making and analysis, office automation and computerised enquiry systems. It is, therefore, not surprising that they did not mention these topics. Expert opinion (both within and outside the civil service), however, indicated that these were the areas where technology was likely to have its greatest impact in the coming years. Indeed, since the time of interviewing (1982/3), there has been a dramatic increase in the number of newer-type applications in the Irish civil service e.g., office automation, networking, spreadsheet

analysis and word processing. These and other
developments in what is known as the "informatics"
field indicated that it would be unwise to limit any
technology-orientated development programme to those
few topics suggested by line managers themselves.

Four Main Themes

In discussions and interviews, managers and
specialists suggested a wide range of possible topics
for inclusion in the proposed development programme.
These suggestions, together with our (albeit limited)
knowledge and understanding of the tasks and
responsibilities managers were likely to have to
undertake in future years, were used to generate a
small number of key subject areas. The following
four themes emerged as being of especial importance
and relevance:

1. Introduction to information technology:
   concepts, uses and organisational
   implications

2. The management and control of computerisation
   projects

3. Strategic planning for information systems

4. Office automation and other "new" technology
   applications.

We recommended that these four themes form the core
content of the proposed technology-orientated
development programme. At a general level, their
selection is easy to justify. To be effective user
managers, Assistant Principal and Principal Officers
will need a reasonably good understanding of computer

concepts and the organisational/human issues associated with the use of technology. Project management and control skills will also be required, especially by managers who have responsibility for heavily computerised areas of work - claims processing, for example. While departmental organisation units most likely will play the dominant role in the development and implementation of medium and long-term technology plans, senior managers in line positions will also be expected to contribute. Again, although managers cannot be expected to keep abreast of technological developments and trends, they should be aware of facilities and applications that probably will affect them directly in the future, such as office automation, microcomputers and electronic funds transfer.

The reasons why each of the above four themes is considered important are discussed more fully in Appendices B-E respectively, which also include a variety of practical suggestions as to how each topic might be covered in the proposed development programme. Figure 1 illustrates some of these proposed learning activities. The remainder of this chapter is concerned with the problem of implementation. In other words, having established the main subjects that ought to be addressed, how should the programme be organised to enable managers learn about these topics?

2.5 Deciding on an Implementation Strategy: The Learning Group Concept

The purpose of most management development programmes is the career development of junior and middle management staff. The aim is to give participants a broad perspective within which to view the job of

Figure 1: Sample Technology-orientated Management Development Programme

Core Topic / Suggested Learning Activities	Introduction to information technology: concepts, uses and organisational implications	Strategic Planning	Project Management and Control	Office Automation and other "new" technology applications
Classroom-orientated activities	Basic foundation course; Presentations and workshops on various topics; Self-paced learning, using video training materials; Vendors' demonstrations; Departmental library	Briefings by experts; Policy workshops	Formal training courses: introductory/appreciation level courses for non-specialist managers; more intensive, in-depth courses for organisation unit staff	Introductory course; Site visits; Demonstrations
Action-orientated activities	Short-term assignments; Site visits; Work-centred projects	Interdepartmental liaison groups	User groups; Short-term assignments	"Hands-on" experience; Pilot projects

management and to provide an overview of many management-related subjects. Participants are usually drawn from different organisations and the programme is conducted externally. While the diversity of participants' organisational backgrounds provides a rich source of material for discussion, it necessarily leads to a certain standardisation of programme content. Such broad-based programmes are useful career development mechanisms for individual officers, but they are less appropriate in situations where the aim is to improve managerial effectiveness rather than managerial knowledge. Recent trends in management development are a departure from the above, rather remote, abstract model towards a specific, focused, experimental approach.[1] Practitioners and theorists are questioning the idea that managerial skill and competence can be taught by conventional training methods, and the emphasis now is on work-centred management development. The main characteristics of this new approach to management development are:[2]

> Programmes run in-house rather than externally
>
> Managers remain as much as possible in the work place, where tutors, trainers and others will come to work with them. As well as being more convenient and less costly for the organisation, this encourages participants to integrate learning with practical experience, and thereby

---

[1] C.J. Margerison, Existential Education, in C. Cox & J. Beck (Eds.), Advances in Management Education, Volume 2, Chichester: John Wiley & Sons, 1983.
[2] G. Wills & A. Day, Buckingham Action Learning Business School: How Well Does the Theory Work? Journal of European Industrial Training, 1984, 8 (6), pp.3-9.

derive the maximum benefit from the development
programme.

Content of programmes tailored to the particular organisation

The programme's content is determined by the
participants' needs and problems. Various
methodologies are used to increase managers'
effectiveness, including conventional "teacher-
tell" methods. Real, rather than artificial,
examples are used wherever possible and every
effort is made to relate teaching materials to
the participants' own experiences at work.

Emphasis on learning rather than training

Programmes focus on the manager as an active
learner responsible for his or her own
development. As far as possible, the programme
shuns the traditional passive learner approach
(i.e., where a trainer tells trainees what they
need to know or should know). The tutor is seen
more as a facilitator or resource person than as
a teacher who is providing prescriptive solutions
to predefined problems. As one management educator
said: "whoever trains, it is only the manager
himself who can learn."[1]

---

[1] Alan Mumford, Self-development for the
     Manager, Personnel Management, 1972, 4, p.33.

Emphasis on applying learning to practice

Programmes emphasise managerial effectiveness
above managerial knowledge. They are geared to
action, and participants work on particular
problems within their organisations. The idea
is to make each manager his or her own
consultant.

Programmes are directed at both the group and the individual

Management requires people to work with and
through other people. For this reason, many
programmes emphasise team development as much as
individual development, encouraging managers
to cross boundaries and gain a wider appreciation
of the total organisation.

None of the above ideas is new. Most can be traced
to the work of Revans on action learning, popularised
in recent years by Foy and Boddy among others.[1]
Although practice lags somewhat behind theory, there
is an emerging body of evidence that demonstrates
the superiority of work-centred management development
over more traditional classroom-based approaches.

---

[1] See for example, R.W. Revans, The Nature of
Action Learning, OMEGA: The International
Journal of Management Science, 1981, 9 (1),
pp.9-24; Nancy Foy, Action Learning Comes to
Industry. Harvard Business Review, September/
October 1977, pp.158-68; D. Boddy, Some Lessons
from an Action Learning Programme. Journal of
European Industrial Training, 1979, 3 (3), pp.
17-21.

Many organisations and management education
institutions have already developed experience-based
programmes, and others are moving towards this
idea.[1] Such programmes have proved particularly
suitable for senior managers - the target group of the
proposed development programme. For these reasons
we recommended that a work-centred approach be used
to improve senior civil servants' technology-related
expertise.

The learning group or learning "set" method was
selected as being the most appropriate. This approach
involves bringing a group of managers together at
regular intervals to discuss work-related issues and
problems and to learn individually and jointly.
Each member of the group, which works with an advisor/
facilitator, is responsible for his or her own
learning and simultaneously acts as a resource to
other group members. The learning group approach is
one of the most successful and popular of the newer
development strategies. It was selected because it
offers a higher degree of flexibility than other
methods - an important advantage when one considers
the demands on senior officers' time. Its major
advantages are: flexibility in terms of membership,
time commitment and the types of learning activities
that are pursued. It also provides a forum for the
exchange of ideas and promotes the idea of learning

---

[1] For example, A.A. Gibb, The Small Business
    Challenge to Management Education. Journal of
    European Industrial Training, 1984, 8 (6), pp.3-9;
    C.E. Kur & M. Pedler, Innovative Twists in
    Management Development. Training and Development
    Journal, June 1982, pp.88-96; Alan Mumford,
    Emphasis on the Learner: A New Approach.
    Industrial & Commercial Training, November 1983,
    pp.342-4.

as a continuous process, for which the learner must take prime responsibility.

(a) Flexibility in terms of membership

Membership of a learning group can be restricted to only one type of manager, e.g., APs and POs with line management responsibility. Alternatively, it can be open to all managers, whether they are line, staff or specialist. It can be a peer group or a mixed-level group, although the former seems to be preferred. Because it is necessary to attend meetings regularly, membership is usually confined to managers from the one organisation; this also promotes group identity and cohesion. Groups of ten or less are the norm, but the level of interest and the motivation of the participants are more important determinants of success than the group's size.

(b) Flexibility in terms of time commitment

Individual members of the group can participate in as many or in as few learning activities as they wish. Organisational crises apart, a member can plan his participation to fit in with the exigencies of his or her day-to-day duties, particular interests or special developmental needs. For example, in a technology-orientated group, some members may wish to concentrate on project control methodologies, others on office automation. Learning activities can be timed to take place at the appropriate moment, e.g., shortly before the start of a

computerisation project or at a particular
stage in that project.

(c)   Flexibility in terms of the types of developmental
      activities pursued

The types of learning activities that are pursued
depend on the nature of the learning goals. For
example, where the goal is defined as cognitive
(i.e., the need for information, facts,
definitions and concepts), the learning
problem is categorised as one of information
transfer and storage.[1] Syllabus-based
programmes and formal training courses have
been found to be effective ways of achieving
this goal. Where the learning goal is
behavioural (i.e., the need for particular skills
and techniques, how-to-do methodologies,
procedures, and so on), such "chalk-and-talk"
methods are much less telling. More practical,
work-centred activities are appropriate in such
circumstances. Within any group, the learning
needs of individual managers are many and varied.
Since some will prefer to learn in a group and
others would rather study alone, a wide range of
learning activities must be offered. In a
technology-orientated programme for Irish civil
servants, for example, some or all of the
following developmental activities might be
included in the group's action plan:

[1] J. Burgoyne & R. Stuart, Implicit Learning
    Theories as Determinants of the Effect of
    Management Development Programmes.
    Personnel Review, 1977, 6 (2), p.5.

- An introductory course for those who have a limited knowledge of information technology

- Individual or group study programmes, using video-based training materials, such as those available from commercial training organisations. These materials are designed for in-house use and can be assimilated by the learner at his or her own pace. They can be used also by groups in tutorials. Managers can choose from a wide range of topics and so can accommodate their learning to their normal working schedule

- Briefings by experts on particular topics

- Briefings by one member of the group to the others

- Vendors' demonstrations

- The setting up of a technology-orientated departmental library, containing books, periodicals, case studies and instructional materials for managers, information on currently available hardware and software products, the names of consultants in the information technology field (including those who have undertaken work for the civil service), details of the kinds of courses and programmes available from external training organisations in Ireland and the UK, and so forth

- Workshops on particular topics, e.g., data security and privacy

- Field trips by one or more members of the
  group to organisations in Ireland or abroad,
  to view systems or processes. The practical
  benefits of these trips are obvious

- The temporary assignment of one or more
  members of the learning group to a project
  team, inside or outside the department, to
  learn at first-hand of the problems and issues
  encountered in developing and implementing a
  computer-based system

- Special projects for members of the group.
  To promote learning and development, such
  projects should address real management
  problems, be concerned with significant
  issues and should lead to corrective action.
  In other words, they should be based on the
  principle of making each manager his or her own
  consultant

- Problem-solving workshops or group sessions,
  in which organisational "veterans" attack
  current departmental problems

- Committee assignments. Appointment of members
  of the learning group to short-term or special
  committees (e.g., on industrial relations
  negotiations vis-à-vis the introduction of new
  technology) where they can get a unique
  vantage-point on a particular issue

- Writing assignments, where the individual
  officer has to do the research, organise the
  data and compile a report that will provide both

needed information and the opportunity for learning

- The organisation of specially designed experimental "learning events", such as role plays, simulations and structured exercises

- Participation by one or more members of the group in outside seminars, training courses, degree or diploma programmes on aspects of information technology

- The formation of internal or interdepartmental user groups to facilitate the exchange of information, ideas and experiences pertaining to computerisation in civil service departments and agencies.

The foregoing list is not exhaustive. It is given by way of example only, to illustrate the variety of learning experiences that can be provided to increase managers' knowledge of and competence in dealing with computer-based systems. To help devise a comprehensive "action learning" plan and to evaluate the results of that plan, experience has shown the importance of having a skilled facilitator — an individual who is at once a member of the group and a trainer.

(d) Provides a forum for the exchange of ideas

There is a great deal of experience of computerisation within the Irish civil service. However, individual experiences are rarely shared within or between departments. A learning group provides managers with a forum within which to

discuss current problems and to share their
distinctive experiences. In a technology-
orientated group, for example, a manager who is
about to become familiar with computerisation
could benefit from the advice and insights of
others who have already been through the process.
In this way, problems might be anticipated and
preventative action can be taken to avoid
problems or errors.

(e) <u>Promotes the idea of learning as a continuous,
active process for which the learner should take
prime responsibility</u>

The idea that people learn best when they take
the initiative has been accepted and practised
for many years in Ireland's primary schools.
It underpins the philosophy of child-centred
education, where the emphasis is on learning by
discovery rather than on learning by rote. The
same principles have been found to hold true of
adult learning, viz., that we learn best when
we are involved directly in real problems to
which the answers are not known. In recent
years, attempts have been made to incorporate
these principles into management education and
training. Project or learning groups have been
a feature of many of these efforts and have
helped managers to <u>learn how to learn</u>. In
particular, they encourage managers:

-   to see the learning process as something
    active and continuous
-   to take responsibility for their own
    learning and to avoid the tendency to

shift responsibility for their development
onto the trainer or teacher
- to become active rather than passive
learners, inside and outside the classroom.

2.6 Key Features of the Proposed Development Programme

The key features of our Phase 1 proposal for a
technology-orientated development programme for senior
managers in the Irish civil service can be summarised
as follows:

- Targeted at assistant principal/principal
  officer level
- Participants drawn from the one department/
  office
- Group-orientated as much as individual-
  orientated
- Content based on four broad themes but tailored
  to meet the requirements and technological
  circumstances of participants and their
  department/office
- Involving a mix of classroom and non-classroom
  learning activities
- Work-centred and geared to issues and problems
  of practical relevance, i.e., rooted in a
  specific organisational context
- Assisted by a group facilitator
- Relatively long-term programme with meetings
  held in-house as far as possible.

The recommendation that the programme focus on a _group_
of managers from the one department was considered
particularly important. It highlighted the fact that
information technology should be viewed as an

organisation-wide phenomenon, requiring the active participation of _all_ senior managers - not just the selected few - if its benefits are to be realised fully.

CHAPTER 3

FROM PROPOSAL TO PRACTICE: EXPERIENCE OF THE
MANAGEMENT INFORMATION TECHNOLOGY LEARNING GROUP

3.1   Formation of a Management Learning Group in the
      Department of Social Welfare

In most fields, the real test of an idea occurs only
when it is put into practice. Given that the Irish
civil service had little or no previous experience
of using an in-house, group learning strategy to
promote management development, it was decided to test
the usefulness of the proposed approach by mounting
a pilot development programme in a selected government
department. The Department of Social Welfare agreed
to participate in the experiment. A group of ten
senior managers (eight Principal and two Assistant
Principal Officers) were invited to form a Management
Information Technology (MIT) learning group in
November 1983.* All accepted and the group's first
formal meeting took place in December 1983. Following
its launch, the MIT group met two or three times every
month from January 1984 to November 1984 (July and
August excepted). The period of the experiment was
therefore long enough to judge the suitability and
effectiveness of the chosen development approach.

---

* A copy of the letter of invitation is contained in
  Appendix F.

3.2 Composition and Computerisation Background of the MIT Group

In 1984, the Department of Social Welfare was structured into five main divisions, as depicted in Table 1. Because of the necessity to limit the size of the group, it was not possible to invite all managers at principal officer level to become members of the group. First preference was given to those managers whose areas of responsibility had been accorded top priority in the Department's computerisation programme. For this reason, Principal Officers in the two main line divisions (Insurance and Assistance) were over-represented in the group. All ten original members were drawn from the four non-computer divisions. An Assistant Principal from the Computer Development Division joined the group four months after the programme had begun. As the programme progressed, some members of the group invited members of their staff (usually Assistant Principals) to attend particular sessions.

When the programme started in January 1984, only two of the original ten members worked in areas where computer systems were a significant factor. Three others worked in sections that were to be computerised within a year or two, three in areas where computer-based systems were planned, and two more in divisions where computerisation was a long-term possibility. Only one of the original group had extensive practical experience of technology-based information systems, having spent some time in the Department's Computer Development Unit. None of the group had any formal systems training.

Table 1: Composition of Management Information Technology Group

DEPARTMENT OF SOCIAL WELFARE	GENERAL DIVISION	PLANNING UNIT	INSURANCE DIVISION	ASSISTANCE DIVISION	COMPUTER OPERATIONS & DEVELOPMENT DIVISION	TOTAL
Total Staff (approx.):	291	27	920	357*	65	1,660
Principal Officers:	4	3	3	3	1	14
Number in MIT Group	2	1	3	2	–	8
Assistant Principal Officers	9	4	8	6	5	32
Number in MIT Group:	1	1	–	–	1**	3

* Excluding approximately 1,000 staff employed in local employment exchanges

** Joined the group one-third of the way through the programme

The group completed a short computer literacy test at the start of the learning programme.* Thirty-three computer concepts were presented and members were asked to rate their current level of understanding on a five-point scale, ranging from "absolutely no knowledge/understanding - have never even heard the term" to "a good knowledge - would feel confident if asked to explain the term to someone else". The maximum possible score on the test was 165 points, the minimum score 33 points.

The results of this test are presented in Table 2. Only one participant rated himself as having a good understanding of most of the computer terms. Another manager understood some terms but overall did not rate himself highly. The remaining eight members had little or no understanding of any of the computer-related concepts.

Table 2: Group Members' Scores on Computer Literacy Test: January 1984. (Self-ratings: Scale = 33-165 points)

	No.
VERY GOOD LEVEL OF UNDERSTANDING (Score > 140 pts.)	1
GOOD LEVEL OF UNDERSTANDING (Score 100-139 pts.)	-
A LITTLE KNOWLEDGE (Score 80-99 pts.)	1
ALMOST NO KNOWLEDGE (Score 66-79 pts.)	3
NO KNOWLEDGE (Score < 66 pts.)	5

---

* A copy of the test is contained in Appendix G.

These scores indicate that, with the exception of
one or possibly two managers, the group embarked on
the learning programme with very little background
knowledge and understanding of information technology.

Levels of interest and motivation, however, were
quite high. All members of the MIT group accepted
that their Department was developing rapidly in the
computerisation field and that, as senior managers,
they would have to participate in the development
and management of these computer systems. The idea
of a technology-orientated management development
programme was probably more appealing than it would
have been in departments where the use of
information technology was only a vague possibility
rather than an absolute certainty. Managers who
know that they will have to cope with computerised
systems in the near future are likely to be more
committed to learning; they are more likely to
persevere and less likely to abandon the programme
after two or three meetings.

3.3   Organisation of the MIT Group Programme

There are essentially three types of learning group:
(a) leader-centred groups, (b) content-centred
groups, and (c) group member-centred groups.[1]
Leader-centred and content-centred groups have much
in common. Both aim to acquire information on a topic

---

[1]   L. Miles and H.W. Stubblefield, Learning Groups
       in Training and Education, Small Group
       Behaviour, 1982, 13 (3), pp.311-20.

for which there is a formal body of practical and theoretical knowledge, both rely heavily on sources external to the group for information and expertise, and both have a designated leader, usually a content expert. In content-centred groups, however, there is much greater concern for group "process", i.e., cultivating a climate of trust and openness and encouraging members to interact with each other and with the "leader". In contrast, group member-centred groups do not meet to acquire knowledge and understanding in the formal sense. They are a variation of the normal management meeting, at which current work problems and issues are discussed. The leader is a "process" expert, not a "content" expert. His or her function is to help the group work together effectively, not to act as a source of information about the subject under discussion. External experts are not used; the group itself is the source of all information. Once the group becomes self-managing, the "leader" or "process" expert withdraws completely.

The MIT group in the Department of Social Welfare was essentially a content-centred group. The objective was to acquire information on a specific topic (information technology) for which a substantial body of knowledge exists. Although members of the group acted as sources of information to one another at various times during the programme, in general external sources were used to improve knowledge and understanding. The leadership role was held jointly by the researcher and an Assistant Principal from the Department's Computer Development Unit, both of whom provided support to the group and undertook all tasks related to the programme's organisation and administration. In the early stages, an external

training consultant from the Institute of Public
Administration helped the group to clarify its
learning needs, and to establish a positive learning
climate.

Ideally, a management learning group should meet once
a week. However, managers' work commitments, and the
fact that the Department of Social Welfare is
geographically dispersed, militated against regular
weekly meetings. A flexible schedule was adopted
and the timing of particular activities was agreed
upon in advance with participants, to minimise
disruption to their departmental duties. This
flexibility was particularly important, given the
volume of work in the Department of Social Welfare and
the fact that much of it is politically sensitive and
subject to continual, critical deadlines. As far as
possible, meetings were held in the Department's main
offices. Site visits were also arranged at convenient
times.

In summary, the main features of the MIT group
programme were:

> - Content-centred on the topic of information
>   technology
> - Conducted in-house
> - Supported by a two-person liaison team
> - Flexible schedule: two or three meetings per
>   month on average
> - Group facilitator, i.e., process expert used in
>   initial stages
> - Reliance for information and expertise on
>   sources external to the group.

3.4 Getting Started

The success of any management development effort
depends on the way it is introduced as much as on
the programme's content. Two factors are of particular
importance here: (i) having the explicit support and
commitment of top management in the organisation, and
(ii) involving participants in the programme's design.
In launching the MIT group programme, particular
attention was paid to both factors.

The opening, critical session was chaired by the
Assistant Secretary with responsibility for computer
development and operations, who stressed the importance
of information technology to the Department, both
currently and in future years. Key problems and
challenges were identified, in particular the need
for good management and effective planning of computer-
based information systems. He welcomed the concept of
a technology-orientated management learning group and
gave top management's support for the MIT group
initiative. This support continued throughout the
period of the programme, and Assistant Secretaries
occasionally sat in on MIT group sessions. This
helped to establish the pilot programme's relevance and
credibility and encouraged managers to take their
participation seriously.

Regarding the second factor - involving managers in the
design process - the perceived learning needs of MIT
group members were identified through a series of
interviews conducted between December 1983 and
January 1984. These were collated by the researcher
and were presented to the group in February 1984. The
members then decided what topics they would like to

cover, and a schedule of learning activities was
drawn up for February-April 1984. This process of
agreeing on topics, scheduling events and reviewing
the value of recent activities was continued throughout
the programme.

3.5 Content of the MIT Group Programme

The programme's content was based on the four broad
areas identified in the earlier phase of the
research: information technology concepts and
implications, strategic planning, project control
and office automation. Managers' own suggestions were
also taken into account. The following list of topics
was derived from interviews with participants:

> Introductory course on basic computer concepts
> Word processing
> Computer graphics
> Computer security and fraud control
> Visit to computer room
> Microfilm
> Facilities offered by An Post
> Introduction to project management
> Using computers to generate management information
> People issues: the ergonomics of workplace design
> Demonstration at VT100 terminal
> Programming in BASIC
> Touchtyping skills.

Perhaps because of the relatively low knowledge base
from which most managers started, they did not
spontaneously mention advanced topics like strategic
planning, database and distributed processing.
However, since planned computer developments in the

Department indicated that such topics ought to be included in a senior management programme, they were added to the above list and discussed with the group at a meeting to decide the programme's general objective. The agreed draft programme incorporated many of the topics that had been suggested by the managers themselves. This ensured that the programme would have a distinctive "Social Welfare" emphasis and would address issues that the management group regarded as relevant.

Appendix H summarises the main learning activities undertaken by the MIT group. Participants' reactions to the programme are discussed in the following section. However, some observations of an evaluative nature are included in the following month-by-month account of the programme.

JANUARY: The programme began with a foundation course. At the time, the Civil Service Training Centre had not yet developed an introductory course for senior managers. A special foundation course was devised by Department of Social Welfare Organisation Unit staff and a senior Central Data Processing Services manager and was presented by them in two half-day modules. The main topics covered were:

1. Information Systems: Theory and Practice
2. The Management Role in Information Systems
3. Technology Concepts and Components:
   - Hardware overview
   - Data storage and management
   - Elementary data communications
   - Security and control
   - Software overview

- Human issues
- Future trends

4. Overview of Data Processing:
   - Batch systems
   - On-line systems
   - Distributed processing
   - Information systems
   - Decision support

5. Data Processing in the Department of Social Welfare
   - Departmental strategy
   - Current systems
   - Planned/future systems

6. User Management Responsibilities:
   - In systems development
   - In systems management.

In addition, MIT group members were given a guided tour of one of the Department's main computer rooms, to reinforce their understanding of the functions of various pieces of computer hardware. Practical demonstrations of some of the Department's main computer systems were also organised so that participants could get a modicum of "hands-on" experience.

Observations: The foundation course served as a refresher course for those managers with some understanding of technology and provided an easy and relatively non-technical introduction for those with a more limited background in computers. The departmental emphasis was particularly well received, and participants found it useful and informative to have current and future systems outlined and discussed in a common forum.

In retrospect, the course was too short. Topics could be discussed only briefly and there was insufficient time to explore the implications of particular issues. However, unlike conventional, once-off computer appreciation courses, it was possible to raise these issues again at later sessions. It would also have been beneficial to have had more "hands-on" experience at this early stage in the programme.

FEBRUARY: Early in the month, the group met to agree a schedule of activities for the following three months. This was an important session. Areas of individual and shared interest were identified, and a draft programme was drawn up with the help of the researcher and a group facilitator. Many of the selected topics would require a great deal of advance preparation and organisation. Some, however, could be covered adequately by site visits, and two such visits were organised shortly after the meeting. Managers were keen to learn about word processing as an aid to efficient administration. A half-day visit to the Civil Service Commission was organised, where the benefits of word processing and list processing were demonstrated. Participants were also shown some uses of optical mark reading (OMR). These demonstrations were very well received, and a second visit was organised later in the programme for those managers who had been unable to attend.

A series of internal demonstrations was also organised in February. The Department's Statistics Unit had developed a number of microcomputer-based financial models that could be used in planning and budgeting. These were used to introduce managers to the concept of decision support systems and to highlight the practical and conceptual problems involved in developing management information and analysis systems.

Observations: Managers' reactions showed that practical demonstrations are a useful and informative means of introducing particular concepts and applications. They are especially relevant when the examples used relate specifically to the managers' own organisation.

MARCH: Members of the group participated in a number of different activities in March. Two managers attended external training courses - one a three-day course in the CSTC and another a 1½-day workshop in the IPA. Most members of the group attended a full-day seminar organised by Digital Ireland, where they heard six presentations on various aspects of office automation and visited an exhibition of information technology products. Some also attended a CSTC-sponsored exhibition in Dublin's Mansion House and a major public exhibition, COMPUTEX, in the Royal Dublin Society.

The group met formally three times: (i) to review the value and usefulness of February's learning activities; (ii) to learn about database, its application, design and implementation, and (iii) to learn about distributed data processing and some of the organisational and management issues that it raises. Commercial video training materials were used in the last two sessions. Their suitability was previewed by an experienced CDPS trainer, who acted as group discussion leader and content expert at both sessions. A senior Departmental computer operations manager also

made a valuable contribution to the session on
distributed data processing. He explained the
various ways in which terminals and computers can be
linked and discussed how the Department planned to
make use of developments in telecommunications
technology to further its computerisation programme.

Observations: Most managers suffered from "information
overload" at the full-day seminar on office automation.
The schedule was very demanding and they were able
to absorb only a small amount of the presenters'
remarks. However, they found the practical
demonstrations excellent. Unfortunately, there was
insufficient time to engage in much practical "hands-
on" experience. Those who attended the CSTC and
COMPUTEX exhibitions did not find them particularly
interesting. The sheer size of COMPUTEX militated
against managers learning anything useful. It
appears that managers need to be accompanied by a
computer expert, if they are to benefit from such
public exhibitions.

In contrast, managers reacted very favourably to the
two in-house sessions on database and distributed data
processing. The input of the experienced CDPS
presenter was the most significant factor here. He
was able to answer managers' questions and to relate
the issues raised in the training tapes to the
particular circumstances in the Department of Social
Welfare. These sessions showed that commercial
training materials can be used in technology-
orientated management training programmes. However,
they should be viewed only as secondary sources of
information, supplementing rather than replacing the
contribution of the content expert. Only managers

with a fairly good background in information technology would be capable of learning from video tapes without the aid of a skilled presenter. Such staff are likely to be found only in departmental organisation and computer development units. Video tapes, nevertheless, offer a readily accessible and relatively cheap source of training materials. They benefit a presenter in structuring a session on a complex topic and should be considered when technology-orientated courses are designed for user managers.

APRIL: Developments in the postal service are of particular interest to the Department of Social Welfare since it transacts over £1 billion worth of business annually through the post office network. MIT group managers were anxious to know what new services An Post was likely to offer in the coming years. An Post responded favourably to a request to speak to the group. A special Social Welfare-orientated presentation was made by a senior manager, who outlined possible developments, including electronic funds transfer, plastic card technology and "smart" card technology. This session was favourably received by the group, and some managers invited their Assistant Principals to attend.

The other main learning activity during April was a half-day session on integrating data processing (DP) and office automation (OA). Commercial video tapes formed part of the input, but the main contributors were two senior CDPS managers. A number of areas in the Department where office automation could be tested on a pilot basis were identified, and the technological, cost and organisational implications of the convergence of DP and OA were outlined.

Observations: The integration of DP and OA was a topic
that managers found it very difficult to understand.
In retrospect, it ought not to have been introduced so
early in the programme. A separate session ought to
have been devoted to the Department's communication
strategy. The integration of DP and OA is a highly
technical subject, not easily grasped by most user
managers. Consequently, it would be advisable to
circulate an easily read handout in advance of such
a session.

MAY: Most of the May activities were devoted to
learning about computer-aided management information
systems. A commercial consultancy firm presented a
special Social Welfare-only seminar on decision support
systems. Several British civil service case studies
were discussed, and various financial models, based
on Social Welfare data, were used to illustrate how
computer graphics can facilitate the presentation of
complex information. On a broader level, the problems
and issues involved in managing and controlling the
quantity and quality of information in an organisation
were outlined by a management services professional
who had experience of working in the civil service.
This latter session was very well received by the MIT
group, as was a presentation by two of the group who
were helping to develop a management information
system for the Department. Since the Department of
Health was also developing such a system, interested
members of the MIT group went on a special visit to
that department.

Also in May, a group member made an informal
presentation on "people issues". This session
focused on the line manager's role in relation to job

design, quality of work environment, staff training
and support, and communications. It was informative
and entertaining.

Observations: Managers' reactions to the decision
support systems seminar were mixed. They found the
content relevant and interesting, but were annoyed at
what one manager termed "the slick, professional
sales pitch approach". This accusation was not
levelled at other external presenters used in the
programme nor at the American managers/actors used in
the commercial video training packages. On balance,
outside presenters add variety and a certain
objectivity to an in-house development programme. In
general, they were well received by the MIT group.
Presentations by one member of the group to the
others were always welcomed; they fostered a sense of
group loyalty and respect and, as such, were
invaluable in developing group identity.

JUNE: During June, some members of the group visited
the Irish Life Assurance Company to review the
usefulness and ease of use of a software package for
describing and automating systems. A second session
was held in October. Although initially managers
found some difficulty in grasping the concepts, the
use of a Social Welfare example to illustrate the
package's capabilities, together with further
practice, helped them considerably.

The main event in June was a session on computer
security and fraud control. A senior auditor from
the Comptroller and Auditor General's Office discussed
the four types of control needed to ensure the
security of systems: organisational controls,

documentation and operating procedures, procedural
controls and management controls. A training video
on computer security supplemented this presentation.
Given the volume of funds disbursed annually by the
Department of Social Welfare, it is not surprising
that members of the group found this session
interesting, informative and relevant. The MIT group
did not meet in July and August. However, some
members of the group agreed to undertake or continue
work on projects related to their own areas of
responsibility during the summer months and to report
on progress later.

SEPTEMBER: Members of the group attended a full-day
workshop on office automation techniques, organised
by Digital Ireland. An Assistant Principal from the
Department of Social Welfare and the researcher acted
as advisors in designing and structuring this
workshop, which was very favourably received. To
avoid problems of "information overload", the workshop
concentrated on only three of the many facilities
available to managers in the area of office automation:
electronic mail, word processing and ADE - a facility
that enables users to develop their own applications.
The workshop involved extensive "hands-on" experience,
and managers had the opportunity to learn at their
own pace, with the help of skilled support staff.

Observations: There was unanimous agreement that the
office automation workshop was excellent, achieving the
right balance between presentation and practice. Any
long programme has its natural ups and downs and the
long summer break caused the MIT group to lose some of
its original momentum. The office automation workshop
was meant to mark the reactivation of the group.

Unfortunately, organisational pressures in September forced half the group to withdraw from the workshop at the last moment, and it was not possible to reschedule it. Consequently, an important, revitalising opportunity was lost at a critical stage in the programme.

OCTOBER: Although the Department of Social Welfare had no plans to computerise its personnel records in the near future, some members of the group were interested in learning how such a system might be developed. AnCO's Computerised Personnel Information System (CPIS) is considered one of the best in the public service. Furthermore, AnCO has approximately the same number of staff as the Department of Social Welfare. Therefore, in October a site visit to AnCO was arranged for interested members of the group. A practical demonstration was organised and the problems, opportunities and benefits of computerising staff records were discussed with two members of AnCO's personnel division. During October, the group met to review progress and to agree on future activities. A half-day seminar was also held on the topic of the manager's role in systems development and implementation. Three speakers from a management consultancy firm took part in this session.

Observations: The AnCO site visit was well received. However, reaction to the systems development seminar was mixed. The main criticism was to do with the style of presentation rather than the content. Since the programme was planned to end in November, most of the October review session centred on managers' opinions of it. Although managers later submitted written comments, this group discussion sparked much useful information of an evaluative nature and was extremely helpful in assessing the programme's strengths and weaknesses.

NOVEMBER: Both learning events in November were on strategic planning. Presenters and participants had raised the importance of planning (in relation to all aspects of organisational functioning) many times during the programme. Two management consultants with extensive experience of the civil service were invited to speak to the group; they had been fully briefed. Strategic planning for information systems was set in the context of overall strategic planning. The important features of strategic planning were outlined and specific techniques and methodologies were explained. This meeting was attended by some non-MIT group managers, including four Assistant Secretaries. Participants agreed that it was an excellent and thought-provoking session and wished to pursue the topic further. A follow-up session was held one week later. The objective of this was to determine the key issues and problems facing the Department, its strengths and weaknesses as perceived by senior management and possible changes/improvements that could be made to increase organisational effectiveness. The researcher who led this session used a non-verbal, "voting with your feet" method, called Meta-Planning, to elicit manager's opinions and suggestions. [1] It worked well and revealed areas where there was group consensus and areas where there was not. A final,

---

[1]   Eberhard Schnell, The Metaplan Method: Communication Tools for Planning and Learning Groups. Metaplan Series, No. 7, Germany: Metaplan, 2085 Quickborn, Goethestrasse 16.

largely social, meeting of the group was held in late
November to mark the end of the pilot programme.

Observations: Although there are individual exceptions,
there is a natural tendency in hierarchical
organisations for the most senior people to dominate
group discussions. In the opinion of the researcher,
this happened at the formal presentation on strategic
planning - Assistant Secretaries contributed more to
the discussion than Principal Officers. The use of a
non-verbal technique in the follow-up session
encouraged all members to contribute and had the added
advantage of generating more ideas and suggestions in
an hour than would be possible in a full-day's
discussion. Although participants had no previous
experience of this technique, they had no difficulty
using it. Perhaps it should have been used at other
MIT group sessions.

Other Inputs to the Programme

Home Computers: Those members of the group who did
not have access to their own computer terminal obtained
access to home computers to increase their awareness of
information technology. Various pieces of business-
type software were also used, as well as computer
data recorders. Although the machines were reasonably
powerful, the quality of the software available left
much to be desired. Personal computers (e.g., IBM PCs,
DEC Rainbows) would have been far superior learning aids
because many high quality and interesting software
packages are available for these machines.

Books and articles: Members of the group were given
books and articles to read at various stages in the

programme. The National Computing Centre's series of
books on computer-related topics was well received
by the group. Although some of these publications were
thought to be too technical, some could be used to
form the nucleus of a user-orientated library.

Teach-yourself-to-type-course: Limited keyboard skills
are required to make the best use of a computer. Few
managers have such skills and find it frustrating and
time-consuming to send even a short message via
computer. To overcome this block, the Department of
Social Welfare installed an inexpensive, teach-yourself-
to-type software package on one of its main computers.
Although this facility was not available all the time
it was a useful learning aid. It encouraged managers to
acquire some limited typing skills in their own time and
at their own pace. In the process, they became
familiar with the computer's operational aspects.

3.6 Evaluation of the MIT Group Programme

The effects of the MIT group programme were felt at both
individual and organisational levels. The programme's
objectives were not quantifiable and so it was not
possible to measure its quantitative effects.
Participation was voluntary. To have introduced formal
assessment where participants might have felt that they,
rather than the programme, were being assessed, might
have jeopardised the exercise.

Nevertheless, evaluation was built into the programme
with a view to obtaining information that would be
helpful in designing future development programmes for
senior civil service managers.

The primary sources of evaulative data were the participants themselves, the researcher, who attended all meetings of the group as a participant observer, and a number of senior staff in the Department of Social Welfare, who were in a position to give an informed judgment on the programme's organisational effects. The participants' views were particularly important, since those who have experienced a programme personally are best placed to judge its strengths and weaknesses.

The MIT group programme was long and placed considerable demands on the managers' time. Consequently, it was not possible to ask participants to give a continuous written response in the form of diaries or essays. To have insisted on such techniques would have meant that most managers would have abandoned the programme. Instead, participants were encouraged to give verbal opinions at review sessions and to express their honest opinions on the worth and usefulness of particular learning activities. These review sessions proved valuable, not only from an evaluative point of view, but also in deciding and structuring future learning activities. To a large extent, the evaluation activity was an integral part of the programme rather than a separate activity. However, in a long programme it is necessary to distinguish between participants' reactions to individual learning events and their opinions of the entire programme. It is also advisable to allow some time to elapse before asking participants for their considered opinions. An evaluation questionnaire was administered six weeks after the group's final meeting, to obtain the members' considered opinions

on the programme's virtues and shortcomings.* The
purpose of this evaluation was to inform rather than
to judge, to discover not only what participants
gained from the programme, but why it had the effects
it did.

Participants' Perceptions of the MIT Group Programme

To gain some initial impressions, participants were
asked to rate the programme as a whole on a number of
7-point rating scales. Figure 2 gives the group's
average rating on each dimension. Managers'
reactions generally were very favourable.

The programme's content was adjudged to be relevant
and interesting, particularly by those managers whose
areas of responsibility were being computerised.
Opinions as to the difficulty of the programme varied
considerably. Those few managers who had a reasonably
good background in information technology found it
easy and intellectually undemanding. However, the
majority found the programme moderately tough and
difficult, especially those with little or no previous
computer experience. This latter group also thought
that the programme's content was significantly more
technical than did other managers.

All participants adjudged the programme to be well-
ordered, fairly active, moderately paced and more
participative than non-participative. Most felt that
it made considerable demands on their time, three
particularly so. In spite of this, all but one felt

* See Appendix I for a copy of this questionnaire.

Figure 2: Participants' Ratings of the MIT Group Programme

Scale: 1   2   3   4   5   6   7

Programme Content:

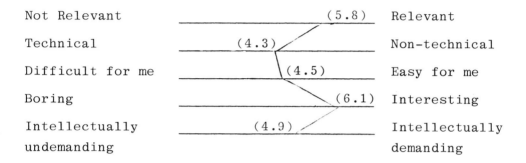

Not Relevant   _____(5.8)___ Relevant

Technical   _____(4.3)_____ Non-technical

Difficult for me   _____(4.5)_____ Easy for me

Boring   _____(6.1)_____ Interesting

Intellectually   _____(4.9)_____ Intellectually
undemanding   demanding

Programme Presentation:

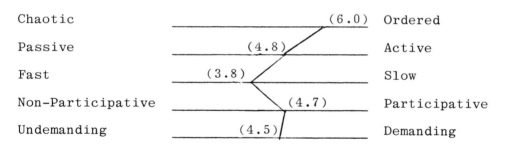

Chaotic   _____(6.0)___ Ordered

Passive   _____(4.8)_____ Active

Fast   _____(3.8)_____ Slow

Non-Participative   _____(4.7)_____ Participative

Undemanding   _____(4.5)_____ Demanding

Overall Evaluation:

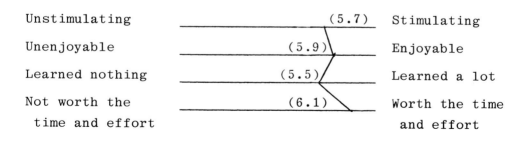

Unstimulating   _____(5.7)___ Stimulating

Unenjoyable   _____(5.9)_____ Enjoyable

Learned nothing   _____(5.5)_____ Learned a lot

Not worth the   _____(6.1)_____ Worth the time
  time and effort   and effort

that their participation had been worth the time and effort. They found the experience enjoyable and stimulating and had learned a reasonable amount about information technology.

3.7   Programme Outcomes

Information technology is a demanding subject and few participants had any background in computerisation. The programme also took up a lot of time. The fact that managers persevered with it over a year indicated that on balance, the programme was seen to be worthwhile. Two further MIT groups (at Assistant Principal level) have since been formed in the Department. The original MIT group has been reconstituted into a Principal Officer Forum, comprising all Principals in the Department. Both these developments can be interpreted as positive indicators of the usefulness of the experimental programme.

Learning Effects

Although no "hard" measures were obtained, Table 3 gives some indication of the programme's learning effects. All managers rated themselves as moving forward on the "computer literacy" continuum - some very much so. Four of the five managers who rated themselves as having "no knowledge" in January 1984 scored themselves as having a "good level of understanding" in January 1985. The fifth manager moved from "no knowledge" to a "little knowledge".

To validate the pre-programme/post-programme comparison, partipants completed the test twice in January 1985: once to assess their current

Table 3: Comparison of Group Members' Scores on Literacy Test: January 1984 v. January 1985

	January 1984	January 1985
VERY GOOD LEVEL OF UNDERSTANDING: (Score > 140 pts.)	1	3
GOOD LEVEL OF UNDERSTANDING: (Score 100-139 pts.)	-	6
A LITTLE KNOWLEDGE: (Score 80-99 pts)	1	1
ALMOST NO KNOWLEDGE: (Score 66-79 pts.)	3	-
NO KNOWLEDGE: (Score < 66 pts.)	5	-
DID NOT COMPLETE TEST	1*	1**
	11	11

*   Manager who joined group in April 1874.

**   Original member of group who did not complete the post-programme test.

(January 1985) level of understanding and once to
assess their January 1984 level of understanding. With
the benefit of hindsight, all but two managers changed
their original pre-programme scores, in the direction
of even less understanding of information technology
concepts.

Attitudinal and Behavioural Effects

Although managers' scores on the computer literacy test
showed that their understanding of computer jargon had
improved considerably, they did not indicate whether
the MIT group programme had any real effects on their
job-related attitudes or behaviour. Managers'
responses to the post-programme evaluation
questionnaire were more revealing and informative in
this regard. These show that participation in the
programme influenced them in several important ways:

- Greater confidence in dealing with organisation
  unit and specialist staff. ("Any vestige of
  awe I might have had for the DP department has
  evaporated.")

- Greater awareness of the need for active user
  involvement in systems design and
  implementation. ("I now realise that the user
  not only can, but must, call the tune if the
  'system' is not to become an end in itself.")

- Reduction of the mystique surrounding computer
  technology in general. ("The myths have been
  dispelled.")

- Increased motivation to learn about technology.
  ("I decided to buy a home computer"; "I
  requested my own personal VDU; I can now

understand the Irish Times computer column
most weeks"; "The MIT group helped me to
follow a pilgrim's path I was going down
anyway.")

- Highlighted the need for a management forum in
  the Department. ("The MIT group hardened my
  resolve to encourage and participate in a
  proper management forum/committee"; "There
  is a need for more open confrontation on the
  various conflicting demands and objectives";
  "A clear statement of corporate strategy is
  needed so that the various sub-plans in the
  divisions dovetail with the overall plan.")

- Greater awareness and more realistic idea of
  what computers can and cannot do. ("I have
  a better idea of what is possible and what is
  not possible"; "I have a better feel for
  computers"; "I am more technically aware.")

- Greater confidence in discussions and meetings
  on technology-related issues. ("I am now in
  a better position to argue the merits of
  particular proposals when dealing with staff
  association demands.")

- Greater knowledge of the Department's computer
  set-up. ("I have a much better idea of the
  workings of the Department's computer regime.")

Organisational Effects

A number of senior managers (including two Assistant
Secretaries) who were not directly involved in the
MIT group programme were interviewed to discover

whether they had perceived any changes in the MIT group managers' job attitudes or behaviour. The main changes instanced were:

- <u>A more positive attitude to computerisation</u>

  In the words of one Assistant Secretary: "The organisational milieu changed noticeably during the year of the programme. Managers were no longer fearful of technology and had overcome their nervousness about working at a computer terminal. Some had requested their own VDU and had become quite proficient at using it."

- <u>Greater user management involvement in computer systems</u>

  Managers were no longer "frightened onlookers", but were anxious and willing to be involved in the design, implementation and management of computer systems. Particular examples were instanced of this greater interest and involvement, e.g., taking the initiative in certain areas, adopting a more critical and questioning approach.

- <u>The development of a healthier relationship between the Department's organisation/ computer development unit and senior line managers</u>

  Line managers and organisation unit staff had a clearer understanding of their different perspectives. Relationships were more open, and a certain "positive tension" had been created as a result of line managers' greater confidence and participation.

- Progress towards the development of an
  effective senior management team

    The MIT group programme contributed towards
    the Department's goal of "creating a harmony
    of minds at senior level". It had also
    helped to integrate managers in geographically
    dispersed locations. The senior management
    forum aspect of the pilot programme was seen
    as particularly beneficial. It was hoped that
    managers would continue to meet regularly
    to discuss organisational problems and issues.

3.8 Programme Costs

Excluding site visits and attendance by individual
managers at external courses, seminars and exhibitions,
the MIT group met 22 times (including the opening and
closing sessions). The main direct financial costs
of the programme were:

Group facilitator fee	£600.00
DELTAK training videos	£770.00*
Fee to outside presenter	50.00
	£1,420.00

* 14 video tapes @ £55 per course month.
  Some of these tapes proved unsuitable and
  were not used in the programme

Ten of the 22 meetings involved only Department of
Social Welfare staff and the researcher: 4 review
sessions, 4 presentations by members of the MIT group,

the official launch and the farewell meeting. Outside
presenters were used for the remaining 12 meetings:
6 civil service presenters (5 CDPS, 1 C & AG) and 6
non-civil service presenters (An Post, Guinness,
Digital and 3 management consultancy firms)   The
cost of outside presenters was a nominal £50 since most
gave their services free-of-charge. In line with
normal practice, no fees were paid to civil service
presenters. The group facilitator attended the
early meetings.

Home computers and reading materials were loaned to the
group. If these were acquired by departments as
learning aids, they would be a once-off cost. Since
they could be used repeatedly, their cost would not
have to be attributed to one programme but could be
set off against a number of programmes. They would,
therefore, comprise a very small proportion of the
total direct costs of any one programme.

Research costs, being development costs, are not
considered a direct cost of the MIT group programme.
To attribute the researcher's full salary to the
programme would give a misleading idea of what it would
cost to mount a MIT group-type programme in another
department.

The cost of the Assistant Principal who liaised with
the researcher is considered a programme cost since
a liaison person would be essential to any MIT
group-type programme. An estimate of this cost,
based on the daily rate for an AP at the mid-point of
the scale, is given overleaf.

Cost of internal liaison person:

Setting up the MIT group   6

Organising sessions, briefing
presenters, liaising with MIT
group and attending sessions.
(5 days a month on average
over 12 months)   60
                                                          ————
                        Total number of days   66
                                                          ————

Daily cost: $\frac{£14,971 + £15,307}{2}$ $\frac{1}{230}$ = £66.00 per day*

Total cost of liaison person = 66 x £66.00 = £4,356

The total cost of the MIT group programme is, therefore
estimated at £5,776 (£1,420 direct costs plus £4,356
for liaison person). This figure divided by 10 gives
an estimated £577 per participant. If apportioned
equally between the 22 meetings of the group, a figure
of £26 per participant per half-day session is derived.
Discounting the fact that Departmental managers
(other than MIT group members) attended a number of
sessions, this cost compares favourably with
conventional training rates.

---

* Average of 3rd. and 4th. points on a 6-point salary
   scale: January 1984 divided by number of working
   days in a year.

- 63 -

The main variable cost in MIT group-type programmes
is the fee of the group facilitator. The experience
of the MIT group shows that such a person can make
a valuable contribution, especially during the
programme's formative stages and at review sessions.
Another variable cost are presenters' fees. The
experience of the MIT group programme shows that civil
service and public service presenters were particularly
well-received. Their knowledge of the civil service
gave them a distinct advantage over private sector
presenters.

As is the case in all management training programmes,
it is relatively easy to measure the costs, but very
difficult to quantify the benefits. The views of
participants and senior management in the Department
of Social Welfare indicated that the programme was
worthwhile and had positive effects individually and
for the organisation. The fact that the Department
has continued with in-house group-orientated
development, by forming two further MIT groups and
continuing the original one, is a clear indicator of
the success of the pilot programme.

3.9 Participants' Evaluation of the MIT Group Concept as a Means of Promoting Senior Management Development

In the post-programme evaluation questionnaire,
participants were asked to reflect on their experience
and to consider the strengths and weaknesses of the
MIT group approach, compared to conventional
management training. Many commented extensively on
this topic. The particular advantages of the MIT
group approach were seen as:

(a)   The departmental focus

Managers felt that the departmental focus
added considerably to the programme's
relevance. It was easier to assimilate
concepts and topics when they were related
to the Department's specific organisational
situation rather than presented in the
abstract. Managers had common interests,
a common vocabulary and, often, common
problems. Detailed descriptions and
explanations were not necessary and it was
easier to "get to the point" or to "make
a point" than on conventional courses, where
organisational differences sometimes hamper
discussion. Managers also felt that the
departmental focus helped to produce a
friendly and relaxed atmosphere. There was
a feeling of "all being in the same boat" and
this resulted in mutual support rather than
rivalry.

(b)   The ongoing nature of the development process

Although some participants found the
programme time-consuming all favoured the
idea of a continuous programme of learning.
One manager said: "MIT was looked upon as
learning and development not training - a
subtle but real difference." And again;
"MIT provided a broader learning experience
than would have been possible on a short
training course."

(c)   The management forum aspect

Although not anticipated, the in-house,
continuing nature of the MIT group programme
filled a vacuum in the Department by
creating the nucleus of a senior management
forum. All participants mentioned this
advantage of the MIT group approach.

(d)   The in-house aspect

All participants felt that holding meetings
in-house was much less disruptive of their
normal work than conventional training. It
also facilitated the simultaneous attendance
of a large number of more senior managers.

(e)   The variety of learning experiences

Managers perceived the MIT group programme to
be more varied than conventional training
courses. It was possible for individual
managers to be selective, to allocate their
time to those meetings and activities that
were considered to be most relevant.
Managers also found it useful to have members
in the group with different levels of
computer experience and expertise. Those
with less experience could learn from those
with greater experience and this gave them
"an added confidence" when dealing with
technology-related issues in their own areas
of responsibility.

The major disadvantages of the MIT group approach, as

compared to management training, were seen as:

(a) Being too available

Managers considered that the major
disadvantage of in-house development was that
participants were readily accessible and
could be "called out at a minute's notice".
This did not happen often with the MIT group,
although occasionally individual managers had
to withdraw from sessions at very little
notice.

(b) "Work" atmosphere

Managers felt that there was no feeling of
"getting away from it all" in in-house
development. The atmosphere was very much a
"work" atmosphere rather than a "training"
atmosphere.

(c) Danger of becoming "incestuous"

Managers felt that in-house programmes could
become "incestuous" unless deliberate
attempts were made to introduce outsiders
from time to time. This external stimulus
was needed to provoke critical thought and
discussion. A major advantage of external
training courses was the opportunity to meet
and talk to people from different backgrounds
and with different perspectives on the same
problem.

On balance, participants favoured in-house development and suggested a number of ways in which the effectiveness of this approach could be improved. They also identified the importance of the group facilitator role. These and other issues are explored further in the next chapter.

CHAPTER 4

REVIEW AND RECOMMENDATIONS

4.1 Ingredients of Success

The experience of the MIT group programme in the
Department of Social Welfare indicates that in-house,
group-orientated management development is a workable
and cost effective method of increasing senior
managers' knowledge and competence of information
technology. However, the Department of Social Welfare
is not a typical government department; it is larger,
more geographically dispersed and more technologically
advanced than most other departments. These factors
were taken into account in designing the programme and
in selecting potential participants. Such an
organisation-specific approach would have to be
adopted if a similar programme were to be mounted in
another department. This said, it is possible to learn
from the MIT group experience, to identify (i) factors
that contributed to its success and (ii) aspects which
should be modified in future programmes.

The main reasons that the MIT programme was received
favourably in the Department of Social Welfare were:

(a) It met a particular learning/development need

(b) It was supported by top management within the
     Department

(c)   It provided a forum for managers at Principal
      level to meet and discuss common organisational
      issues and problems

(d)   The general approach proved to be suitable to the
      topic under discussion.

To the extent that similar conditions exist in other
departments, the prognosis for MIT group-type
programmes is good.

(a)   The programme met a particular learning/
      development need

      The Department of Social Welfare had reached a
      stage in its development when some form of
      technology-orientated training for managers was
      necessary. It was not difficult to motivate the
      participants. All managers recognised the
      necessity for their active participation in
      learning more about computer systems. Such might
      not be the case in other less technologically
      advanced departments. Few senior managers in any
      organisation, public or private, are interested
      in learning for learning's sake. They will commit
      time and energy to learning only if it can be
      shown to be of practical relevance to their
      present or future work.

      To excite interest and commitment, a programme
      must fall into the "need-to-know" category rather
      than the "nice-to-know" category. Information
      technology provided the key in the Department of
      Social Welfare. Different topics are likely to
      be of greater interest and relevance in other
      departments. The MIT group programme

demonstrated that managers will respond
positively to a programme if they think that it
is congruent (in timing and subject-matter) with
their real development needs.

(b)   The programme was supported by top management
within the Department

The interest and support of senior managers is a
critical factor in all management development
efforts.   The MIT group programme was fortunate
in this regard.   Top management support was
visible and positive and contributed towards
participants agreeing to take part in the
programme.

(c)   The programme provided a forum for Principal
Officers to meet and discuss organisational
issues and problems

Although technology provided the initial catalyst
to participation, the opportunity to meet
regularly with other senior managers significantly
contributed to continuing participation in the
programme.   If a similar programme was mounted in
another department, this aspect could be stressed
even more strongly.   The MIT programme was as
much an organisation or group development
programme as an individual programme.   In
reviewing it, participants were asked about the
composition of the management learning groups.
The majority favoured peer-level over mixed-level
groups.   However, the MIT group was essentially
a Principal Officer group and the special needs
and problems of mixed-level groups did not form

part of the research programme. Consequently,
we can only recommend that the question of group
composition should be given serious consideration
in mounting any in-house development programme for
senior managers.

(d)   The general approach proved to be suitable to the
      topic under discussion

      More than most subjects of interest to senior
      managers, information technology needs to be set
      in a particular organisational context if managers
      are to understand the complex and often wide-
      ranging implications of its use in organisations.
      Consequently, the largely in-house, departmentally
      focused approach used in the MIT programme proved
      particularly appropriate to technology-orientated
      learning.

.2   Review of the Programme's Content

Aspects of the programme that could be improved upon
were identified in the previous chapter's month-by-
month account of the MIT group programme. These are
explained more fully below, and further suggestions
put forward by participants are set out:

        -   Earlier and more extensive "hands-on"
            experience

            Having access to a computer adds
            immeasurably to the quality of each manager's
            learning experience. At the very least,
            participants should be given access to home
            computers, or preferably micro-computers.

Some MIT group participants suggested a "computer laboratory", where managers could work informally to familiarise themselves with various types of computers and software packages. A variation of this concept (a micro-computer support centre) has since been established in the Department of Finance.

- **A good foundation course for those with little or no background in information systems**

    This shortcoming in the original MIT programme has since been rectified with the development of a foundation course by the Civil Service Training Centre. The course has proved successful with subsequent management learning groups in the Department of Social Welfare.

- **Greater emphasis on project work; greater demands on participants**

    The original blueprint for a technology-orientated management development programme envisaged that it would be intensive and demanding. However, a less taxing, more cautious approach was adopted in designing the MIT programme. The feeling was that a less ambitious programme would be more suitable, given the demands on senior officers' time and their relative lack of experience of formal management development. The need to encourage wide participation and

prevent the MIT programme from becoming
a vehicle for "preaching to the converted"
were also significant factors. For these
reasons, project work was not mandatory,
nor were participants obliged (unless they
so wished) to make presentations or
undertake reading assignments. Nevertheless,
many did so. However, some MIT group
managers felt that more should have been
asked of participants; they recommended
that future programmes should place greater
demands on managers, e.g., all group
members should make informal presentations
and should undertake technology-orientated
project work in their own areas of
responsibility. Greater and more durable
individual learning effects could be
expected from such a programme. However,
possible adverse organisational
consequences (e.g., fewer managers "staying
the course", the unintentional creation of a
computer elite) should also be considered in
the design of future development programmes.
In most circumstances, it should be possible
to strike a middle path, i.e., a programme
that places greater personal demands on
participants than the MIT programme, but
which does not interfere unduly with a
manager's normal work.

4.3 Review of the Programme's Organisation

The comments of the MIT group mangers on the
organisational aspects of the programme indicated that
they were very satisfied. They did not suggest any

radical changes to the basic format. Among the aspects that they felt should be retained for future programmes were:

- In-house meetings as far as possible
- Meetings during normal working hours
- Half-day sessions, with occasional full-day sessions
- Sessions held as far as possible at the same time on the same weekday (e.g., 9.30.a.m. on Wednesdays)
- The occasional use of outside presenters to broaden persepectives and to stimulate ideas
- Site visits and video training materials, where appropriate
- The services of a group facilitator/organiser.

MIT group managers indicated that a group facilitator influences the development programme in several ways:

- As a group formation/team building agent, encouraging individuals to join and then to feel part of the group

- As a motivator, encouraging members to persevere with the programme even when their interest is waning

- As an informal leader/coordinator at meetings, asking questions and encouraging members to contribute

- As a resource person, identifying and reviewing the suitability of various training materials, establishing contact with and briefing presenters.

All MIT group members thought that the group
facilitator ideally should be someone from outside the
department. Credibility, perceived expertise,
objectivity and the "embarrassment factor" were cited
as an outsider's main advantages.

It was argued that most departmental training officers
(the natural choice for an in-house facilitator) would
not have the credibility, status or expertise
effectively to manage a Principal Officer learning
group. There was also a belief that a departmental
facilitator would have less time to devote to a
learning programme than an outsider, i.e., time to
prepare for meetings, to establish and liaise with
external presenters, and so on. He or she would
inevitably be drawn away to other duties. Again,
participants said that there was a very real danger
that if a programme was organised internally, it would
become identified solely with the section that had
organised it (e.g., Training, R & D, Organisation
Unit), and consequently it would lose its broader
organisation-wide management orientation. The
"embarrassment factor", was articulated by several
managers, e.g.: "It would be much easier to give in to
work pressures and absent oneself from meetings if one
of our own was involved"; "An outsider gets more
respect and commitment."

In the final analysis, it was thought that the
facilitator's personal qualities are more important
than the organisation from which he or she comes.
As one manager said "The key question is: has the
person the qualities and competence necessary for the
task?" Or again: "The person, not the source is the
important factor.... he/she must have the right

personality and abilities."

4.4   Practical Recommendations

Recommendations, suggestions and guidelines as to how
senior civil service managers might be helped to
acquire the knowledge and skill needed to plan and
manage computerised information systems effectively
are contained in both the body and appendices of this
report.   The major recommendations are:

1.   All departments

Technology-orientated management development
programmes should be undertaken in all government
departments.   Priority should be be given to those
departments or agencies where technological
developments are already proceeding (or are likely
to proceed) fairly rapidly.

2.   In-house

As far as possible, these programmes should be
conducted in-house to make it easier for a large
number of senior officers to attend.

3.   Group-orientated

The programme should be tailored for groups as
much as for individuals.   The prime objective
should be the development of a cadre of informed
senior managers rather than the development of a
few selected individuals.

4.   Long-term

The programmes should be viewed as long-term
development efforts rather than as singular
training courses. This is not to say that
conventional training courses have no place in the
programmes; rather, that training courses be
presented as part of a total programme and not
as the sole response to managers' learning needs.

5.   Foundation course

A foundation course (conducted in-house if
possible) should be used to start these longer
term programmes in participating departments.

6.   Target group

The target group for the programmes should be
non-specialist senior managers (Assistant
Principal and equivalent and upwards). The more
technical and specialised learning needs of
managers in organisation and computer development
units should be addressed separately.

7.   Group size

The size of the group should be limited generally
to 10-12 senior managers.

8.   Group composition

While mixed-level groups (AP/PO, PO/Assistant
Secretary) may be appropriate in certain
circumstances, the experience of the MIT group

experiment in the Department of Social Welfare
indicates a higher degree of acceptance for peer-
level (or predominantly peer-level) groups.

9.   Non-technical focus

The programmes should focus on the user manager's
role in systems planning, implementation and
management. The emphasis should be on the
"what" and "why" aspects of information technology
rather than on the "how" features.

10.   Context-specific

Differences in function, experience of
computerisation and probable future developments
should be taken into account when a technology-
orientated programme is devised for a particular
department. Real, rather than artificial,
examples should be used whenever possible and
every effort should be made to relate concepts
and teaching materials to the particular
circumstances of the participating department
and to the managers' own work experiences.

11.   Areas of overlap

While a certain amount of tailoring will be
required to achieve the correct programme content,
it is likely that the technology-related learning
needs of managers in different departments will
be similar in many respects. The extent of this
overlap should be investigated to determine those
content areas where the demand for training is
greatest. Materials should then be developed

for use in several programmes.

12. Panel of civil service presenters

The use of non-civil service presenters and
content experts will sometimes be both necessary
and desirable. However, civil service presenters
should be used wherever possible. A panel of
content experts on technology-related topics
should be formed from which presenters could be
drawn.

13. Use of internal staff as presenters

Departments should be encouraged to use internal
presenters and discussion leaders (including
participants themselves) in their senior
management development programmes.

14. Interesting sites

Visits to organisations that have made progress
in computerised information systems should form
part of the development programmes. A list of
such sites in the civil service and the wider
public service should be drawn up.

15. Office automation pilots

Carefully chosen and managed office automation
pilot projects should be undertaken to provide
first-hand experience of the problems and
opportunities posed by advanced information
systems.

16. Strategic planning

The Department of the Public Service has prepared
guidelines for information technology planning.
Inter-departmental liaison groups at (a) top
management level and (b) senior organisation/
planning unit level should be formed to discuss
strategic planning issues. Policy workshops, both
service-wide and departmentally based, should be
organised to help departmental senior management
produce strategic plans for information systems.

17. Guidelines and standards

Guidelines and standards for user management
training should be drawn up to ensure high-
quality development programmes.

The theme underlying many of the above recommendations
is that current facilities for management development
in the field of information technology in the civil
service need to be expanded. In particular, there is
a need for (a) greater flexibility, (b) more active
experimentation, and (c) a greater emphasis on
organisation development (as opposed to individual
manager development). Implementating these changes
will require a changing and even more developmental
role for the training function in Ireland's civil
service.

GLOSSARY OF COMPUTER TERMS

BATCH PROCESSING: A processing mode in which records of a
   similar kind (e.g., salaries) are collected periodically
   (e.g., weekly), processed in a reasonably generous time-
   span (e.g., overnight) and the whole process repeated the
   following week or month. This method of processing is in
   contrast to ON-LINE PROCESSING.

BUBBLE MEMORY: Memory is which data are stored on moving
   bubbles of magnetism on a semiconductor.

CATHODE RAY TUBE (CRT): The screen or display component of
   a computer configuration. Synonymous, though not
   technically identical, with a video display unit or
   monitor.

CENTRAL PROCESSING UNIT (CPU): The computer's brain which
   carries out logic and arithmetic functions and
   supplies control signals.

CHIP: A small wafer of silicon or other semiconducting
   material, containing a large number of circuits for
   storing and processing information.

COM: Computer Output Microfilm.

CONFIGURATION: The arrangement of the physical components
   of a computer system.

CONVERGENCE: The coming together of computers,
   telecommunications and office equipment.

DAISY WHEEL: A printer type-head, in which the characters
   are located at the tips of flexible stalks radiating from
   a centre.

DATABASE: A computer system holding large amounts of data
   in a consistent manner.

DECISION SUPPORT SYSTEMS: Information systems designed to
   assist professional and managerial decision-making.

DIANE: Direct Information Access Network for Europe.
   An on-line information service, opened in 1979 and
   controlled by the European Commission.

DIGITAL COMMUNICATIONS: Sending messages by means of
   strings of discrete and separate values, using zeros and
   ones.

DISC: A magnetic recording medium on which information
   may be read or written in digital code.

ELECTRONIC FUNDS TRANSFER SYSTEMS (EFTS): Banking systems
   that use electronic rather than paper means of
   transferring money between accounts.

ELECTRONIC MAIL: A means of distributing addressed
   messages electronically.

EXPERT SYSTEMS: Programs that can assimilate and
   structure information about a narrow range of
   expertise, and then provide expert advice.

FACSIMILE TRANSMISSION (FAX): A means of transmitting a
   facsimile copy of a document or diagram via a
   communications line.

FIFTH GENERATION: There have been three distinctly
   recognisable generations of computers, based respectively
   on valves, transistors and integrated circuits. The
   fourth generation, much less clearly defined, is based on
   very large-scale integration (VLSI). The Japanese

Information Processing Development Centre has framed requirements for the fifth generation up to ten years in advance.

GRAPHICS: Normally refers to computer software that is used to create and manipulate drawings on a screen.

HARD COPY: A document produced on paper, as opposed to magnetic or electronic media.

HARDWARE: The various mechanical, electrical, electronic and magnetic parts of a computer. Contrasted with software.

INPUT/OUTPUT DEVICES: The devices used to get information into and out of a computer e.g., keyboards, printers and so on.

INTERACTIVE: A system that acknowledges and responds quickly to user commands, giving two-way communication.

LANGUAGE: The means used by a programmer or user to communicate with a computer. A low-level language is close to what the computer can directly understand. A high-level language (often resembling English) is more user-orientated or "user friendly".

LINEPRINTER: A high-speed printer that prints a complete line at a time.

LOCAL AREA NETWORK (LAN): A cheap, powerful and flexible means of connecting microcomputers and other items of office equipment.

MAINFRAME COMPUTER: A large, powerful computer, traditionally used for large-scale data processing.

MICROCOMPUTER: A small, cheap computer, based on a microprocessor.

MICROGRAPHICS: The generic term for microfilm, microfiche, COM etc.

MICROPROCESSOR: The central processing unit of a computer, implemented on a single silicon chip.

MINICOMPUTER: Originally, a computer significantly smaller in size and capacity than a mainframe. Technical advances have largely blurred the distinction.

MIS: Management Information Systems.

OPTICAL CHARACTER READING (OCR): A photoelectronic means of recognising alphanumeric characters which have been machine printed using a single type face or font.

OPTICAL MARK READING (OMR): A photoelectronic means of recognising markings on paper or other substances. Used in correcting multiple-choice examination papers and identifying the prices of items in supermarkets etc.

ON-LINE PROCESSING: A mode of processing in which terminals are connected to a computer, giving a rapid response to user commands, in contrast to batch processing.

PABX: Private Automatic Branch Exchange. An internal telephone system connected to the public telephone network.

PACKET SWITCHING: An efficient method of transmitting 'packets' of information over a telecommunications network.

PERIPHERALS: Items of equipment connected to a computer system, e.g., disc drives and printers.

PRESTEL: A proprietary Viewdata system marketed by British Telecom.

PTT: Post, Telegraph and Telephone Authority.

SEMICONDUCTOR: A material that conducts electrical current when the voltage across it is above a certain level. It acts as a resistor when the voltage is below that level.

SHARED LOGIC: A wordprocessing system in which the central
   processor and/or peripherals are shared by a number of
   screens.

SOFTWARE: All the computer programmes associated with a
   computer system.

STAND-ALONE SYSTEM: A self-contained wordprocessing or
   other computer system, not connected to any other
   hardware.

TELECONFERENCING: Three-way (or greater) communication by
   telephone.

TELETEX: A worldwide electronic mail service provided by
   PTT authorities.

TELETEXT: Videotext services provided by television
   broadcasting authorities.   Inherently less interactive
   than viewdata.

TIMESHARING: A system in which CPU time and system
   resources are shared between a number of tasks.

VIDEO DISPLAY UNIT (VDU):   A screen used to display data,
   text or graphics in a computer or wordprocessing system.

VIDEOTEX/VIDEOTEXT: The generic term for viewdata and
   teletext systems, allowing access to databases via
   modified television sets and/or the telephone service.

VIEWDATA: Videotext services provided by telecommunications
   authorities.

WORDPROCESSING: The application of computer technology to
   the storage and manipulation of text.

WORKSTATION: A computer terminal, consisting of a screen,
   a keyboard and possibly several other components.

BIBLIOGRAPHY

ARANDA, R.R. (1969), Personal Computers as Work Stations. Proceedings of the Digital Equipment Computer Users Society: St. Louis, Missouri, May 1969.

BARRON, I. and R. CURNOW (1979), The Future with Microelectronics. Milton Keynes: Open University Press.

BIRCHALL, D.W. and V.J. HAMMOND (1981), Tomorrow's Office Today. London: Business Books.

BODDY, D. (1979), 'Some Lessons from an Action Learning Programme,' Journal of European Industrial Training, 3 (3), pp.17-21.

BROOKS, F.P. (1979), The Mythical Man-Month. Reading, Massachussetts: Addison-Wesley.

BURGOYNE, J. and R. STUART (1977), 'Implicit Learning Theories as Determinants of the Effect of Management Development Programmes,' Personnel Review, 6 (2), pp.6-14.

CENTRAL COMPUTER AND TELECOMMUNICATIONS AGENCY (1980), New Office Technology in the Civil Service. London: CCTA.

CENTRAL COMPUTER AND TELECOMMUNICATIONS AGENCY (1984), Information Technology in the Civil Service: Early Experience with Multi-User Office Systems. Information Technology Series, No. 7. London: HMSO (CCTA).

COMPUTER TALK, March 22 1982.

COMPUTING, March 4 1982.

COOPERS AND LYBRAND ASSOCIATES LTD. (1983), Deciding Information Strategy. Dublin: Paper presented to the Department of the Environment.

DEPARTMENT OF THE PUBLIC SERVICE (1984), Office Automation in the Civil Service: What Managers Need to Know. Computer exhibition leaflet. Dublin.

DIEBOLD, J. (1979) Forward to the Diebold Group Special Report, Information Resource Management: New Directions in Management, Infosystems, October 1979.

DRUCKER, P. (1979), Management: Tasks, Responsibilities, Practice. London: Pan Books.

FOY, N. (1977), 'Action Learning Comes to Industry,' Harvard Business Review, September/October, pp.158-68.

GIBB, A.A. (1984), 'The Small Business Challenge to Management Education,' Journal of European Industrial Training, 8 (6), pp.3-9.

HEARSON, P. (1982), 'Systems Training in the Civil Service College,' Management in Government, pp.34-7.

HOSKYNS, Ltd. (undated), Project Management Course Notes: Project Planning and Control Principles. J. Hoskyns & Co. Ltd., London.

JAPANESE INFORMATION PROCESSING DEVELOPMENT CENTRE (1981), Preliminary Report on Study and Research on Fifth Generation Computers. Japan: JIPDC.

KUR, C.E. and M. PEDLER (1982), 'Innovative Twists in Management Development,' Training and Development Journal, June, pp.88-96.

LOCK, D. (1977), Project Management (2nd. edition). Farnborough, Hants.: Gower Press.

MARGERISON, C.J. (1983), 'Existential Education', in C. Cox and J. Beck (eds.), Advances in Management Education, Volume 2. Chichester: John Wiley & Sons.

MARTIN, J. (1981), Applications Development without Programmers. Englewood Cliffs, New Jersey: Prentice-Hall Inc.

MILES, L. and H.W. STUBBLEFIELD, 'Learning Groups in Training and Education,' Small Group Behaviour, 13 (3), pp.311-20.

MUMFORD, A. (1972), 'Self-development for the Manager,' Personnel Management, 4 pp.30-3.

MUMFORD, A. (1983), 'Emphasis on the Learner: A New Approach,' Industrial and Commercial Training, November, pp.342-4.

MUMFORD, A. and D. HENSALL (1979), A Participative Approach to Computer Systems Design. London: Associated Business Press.

NETHERLANDS SOCIETY FOR INFORMATICS (1981), User Training Working Party, Education Section, User Training: What Should the User Know? Amsterdam: NSI.

NOLAN, R.L. (1979), 'Managing the Crisis in Data Processing,' Harvard Business Review, March-April, pp.115-26.

PRICE, S.G. (1979), Introducing the Electronic Office. Manchester: National Computing Centre.

REVANS, R.W. (1981), 'The Nature of Action Learning,' OMEGA: The International Journal of Management Science, 9 (1), pp.9-24.

SCHNELL, E. (undated), The Metaplan Method: Communication Tools for Planning and Learning Groups, Metaplan Series,

No. 7. Germany: Metaplan, 2085 Quickborn, Goethestrasse 16.

SYNNOTT, W.R. and W.H. GRUBER (1981), Information Resource Management: Opportunities and Strategies for the 1980s. New York: Wiley.

TAYLOR, F.W. (1911), The Principles of Scientific Management. New York: Harper and Row.

THOMPSETT, R. (1980), People and Project Management. New York: Yourdon Press.

WILLS, G. and A. DAY (1984), 'Buckingham Action Learning Business School: How Well Does the Theory Work?' Journal of European Industrial Training, 8 (6), pp.3-9.

WYLIE, R. (1975), Project Planning and Control for Data Processing. Manchester: National Computing Centre.

YOURDON, E. (1982), Managing the System Life Cycle. New York: Yourdon Press.

APPENDIX A

Report of Research Workshop:
"Senior Civil Servants and
Information Technology:
Pathways to the Future"

Purpose of Workshop

The workshop was organised by the Research Division of the Institute of Public Administration. It formed part of the process of identifying how best to prepare senior civil servants for the challenges of information technology. The main purpose of the workshop was to provide a forum in which discussions could take place between user managers, computer specialists, the research team and other interested parties. The focus of the discussion was on the practical problems facing non-specialist managers who have responsibility for the development and operation of computer-based information processing systems.

Summary of Discussion

The main points raised by participants at the workshop were:

The urgent need for some form of technology-orientated development programme for non-specialist managers

User managers agreed that they were at present inadequately prepared for their computerisation responsibilities. All thought that experience was the only real teacher. However, most felt that more formalised training could be beneficial, especially if it was undertaken immediately before they took part in a computerisation project.

Fear as a motivator

The user managers' desire for some form of development

programme was <u>motivated primarily by feelings of fear</u>
or inadequacy, i.e., fear of not knowing what was
going on, fear of not being able to keep track of and
control developments for which they were responsible,
fear of being forced to abdicate responsibility to
computer specialists. As stated by one workshop
participant:

> Many managers feel psychologically
> disadvantaged when dealing with
> specialists because of their own
> lack of knowledge and skill.

They felt that participation in a development
programme would help reduce, if not eliminate, these
feelings of psychological disadvantage. The following
comment by one manager expressed the general feeling:

> Managers need to lose their fear
> of technology. They need to have
> enough knowledge to be able to know
> what questions to ask, to be aware of
> the capabilities and potential of
> computers and to be able to attempt
> to evaluate alternatives themselves.

Time as the user manager's greatest enemy

User managers indicated that it would be impossible
for them to participate in any development programme
that took up a lot of their time. They advocated
short, intensive training or learning experiences,
which could be fitted into the normal, busy working
schedule of line managers at Assistant Principal and
Principal Officer level. Many stressed that
development had to be a sustained effort, not just
a "once-in-a-blue-moon thing". They supported the
idea of a modular-type development programme.

Subject areas to be covered in the development programme

Managers found it very difficult to identify specific topics that they would like to see included in a technology-orientated development programme, despite the fact that all workshop participants had been or were currently involved in large-scale computerisation projects. They had never thought of computerisation in terms of their own or their staff's training and development needs. However, two subject areas were mentioned consistently as meriting inclusion in a technology-orientated development programme: (a) explanation of computer concepts and jargon and (b) project management and control techniques. Line managers felt that training or instruction in these two fields would be welcomed by Assistant Principal and Principal Officers before they took part in a computerisation project. They considered that such training would increase the confidence of managers in their ability to supervise the transition from manual to computerised systems of work. Other topics recommended by individual officers were: the explanation of concepts employed in systems analysis, how to conduct a feasibility study, and project budgeting and costing techniques.

The user manager's abilities are only one factor determining the success of computerisation projects

Participants stressed that the line manager's competence was only one factor contributing to a project's success or failure. They cited other factors as being more critical, principally:

- the quality of and the amount of time spent on planning

- the speed of decision-making

- the level of support from top management.

User managers said that many of the problems that were experienced in implementing computer systems could be traced to a lack of planning or to hasty planning. Fewer problems had been encountered in projects that had enjoyed a relaxed planning phase.

Users and computer specialists had had time to discuss requirements and potential problems. The slowness of decision-taking was also criticised; too much time was spent reaching decisions and this led to delays and other problems. Difficulties mostly were avoided where top management was supportive and well-informed about the issues involved in computerisation. Many managers thought that some form of education/awareness programme for top management (Assistant Secretaries/Secretary) was necessary.

<u>Need for a joint development programme for user managers, computer specialists and staff in departmental organisation and planning units</u>

The participants in the workshop thought that the relative roles of the user manager, the computer specialist and staff in departmental organisation and planning units should be clarified. The line manager could not and should not be expected to become an expert on computerisation; this was the

function of the specialist, not the generalist,
manager. Effective user-specialist relationships
depended as much on the specialist as on the user.
It was not simply a matter of the user manager
learning to ask the right questions. There was an
equal onus on specialist staff to volunteer
information and advice. For this reason, a joint
development programme for both line managers and
specialist staff (computer, organisation and
planning) was more likely to lead to better
communication than one aimed solely at line managers.

Need for departmental planning in relation to information technology

Apart from the question of planning for individual
projects, participants maintained that there was a
real need for some form of department-wide plan
regarding the future development and use of computers.
Such strategic planning should be the responsibility
of top management, they thought, although all senior
officers (both line and specialist) ought to be
involved in the policy-making process.

Need for technology-orientated training to be rooted in a civil service context

Participants stressed the need for technology-
orientated management development to be set firmly
in the context of the Irish civil service. The
content of development programmes would have to be
tailored to suit the civil service; sending individual
managers on computer appreciation courses offered by
commercial training agencies should not be viewed as
an adequate response to the development needs of civil
service managers.

Theme 1: Introduction to Information Technology:
Concepts, Uses and Organisational Implications

The Need for an Introductory Course on Information Technology

Senior managers' knowledge of information technology, its uses and probable organisational implications is currently very limited. Few (apart from computer specialists and some organisation unit staff) have more than a superficial understanding of basic computer concepts and terminology. Most would welcome some form of introductory or foundation course. Such a course should be viewed as only the first step in technology-orientated management training and not as the sole response to managers' learning needs. It should be presented as part of a longer term programme of development and ideally, should, involve site visits, demonstrations and "hands-on" experience, besides attendance at formal presentations.

The Content and Delivery of an Introductory Course

Three sources were of particular benefit in determining what non-specialist managers needed to know about information technology: (i) senior specialist staff in the civil service, (ii) the content of various commercially available training programmes and packages aimed at user managers, and (iii) the recommendations of the User Training Working Party of the Education Section of the Netherlands Society for Informatics (NSI). [1]

---

[1] Netherlands Society for Informatics, User Training Working Party, Education Section, User Training: What Should the User Know? Amsterdam: Netherlands Society for Informatics, 1981.

Specialist staff in the civil service suggested that the
following eight topics were essential for user managers:

    Computer hardware

    Computer software

    Approaches to data processing (DP)

    Design and analysis of systems

    System security and control

    Project management: user manager responsibilities

    Staff control

    Support services: technical and non-technical.

A similar list emerged from a review of the content of
several commercially available user manager-orientated
training courses. No two courses were identical. However,
the following six subject areas occurred with such
frequency as to appear to be the core topics for inclusion
in any introductory course for non-technical managers:

    Computer hardware

    Computer software

    Approaches to data processing (DP)

    System security and control

    Systems development and implementation

    Role and responsibilities of user managers.

Unlike the previous two sources, the NSI User Training
Working Party was concerned with defining an ideal,
comprehensive curriculum or information set for users.
Therefore, their list of topics is much more detailed. They
identify twelve major subject areas, each of which is broken

down into a number of sub-categories. The twelve major
areas are:

General aspects of automation

Organisational aspects of automation

Information and information analysis

The functional layout of an application system

The technology and applicability of technical aids

People involved in automation

The development of an application system

The management of an application system

Automation in the user's own organisation

Programming by the user

Social aspects of automation

Special subjects (e.g., office automation,
graphics).

Following a review of these sources, a possible curriculum
was drawn up for a foundation course for senior managers.
Training materials that could be used in developing such
a course were also identified. The following five topics
formed the basis of the recommended curriculum:

1. Computerisation in the Irish Civil Service

- An overview of the current situation and planned
  future developments in relation to information
  technology in the civil service
- A discussion of such issues as the centralisation/
  decentralisation of computer facilities and the
  changing roles and responsibilites of departmental

line managers vis-à-vis the management and
control of technology.

2. Information and Information Analysis

    - The need for line departments to identify their
      information requirements before they embark upon
      or intensify their computerisation programmes.
      The role of line managers in this identification
      process

    - Introduction to information as a concept, the
      many forms it can take, the uses to which it can
      be put, and the processes by which it is produced
      in departments

    - The need for congruence between organisational
      structures and information systems.
      Modifications may be needed in both to facilitate
      computer-based information systems.

3. Technology: Concepts and Components

    - Introduction to hardware and software concepts
    - Advantages/disadvantages associated with
      particular technical options from a manager's
      standpoint, e.g., costs, speed, reliability
    - Introduction to the types of computer
      applications available currently.

4. Approaches to Data Processing

    - Alternative DP approaches (batch, on-line) from
      a practical rather than a technical point of
      view.

5. <u>Tasks and Responsibilities of User Manager</u>

- Manager's responsibilities at each stage of the systems development process: initial study, specifying requirements, design, development, testing, implementation, running and review

- Systems security and control

- Privacy and confidentiality of data

- Motivation and training of staff

- Project management aids

- Why things go wrong: typical problems and how they are handled.

Since the presentation of this curriculum, a three-day foundation course on information technology has been developed for senior officers by the Civil Service Training Centre in Dublin. The course covers most of the afore-mentioned topics and, in addition, incorporates extensive "hands-on" experience at a micro-computer. The course covers basic computer concepts and terminology; a survey of the type of advanced information technology systems currently on the market; current developments in the civil service; productivity and other implications of the new information technologies and the roles and responsibilities of user managers in relation to technology.

Were such a foundation course to be organised on a departmental basis, it would provide a logical and useful starting point for technology-orientated management development. Senior managers from the participating department could be invited to attend and, where possible, the course could be conducted internally. In certain instances, minor modifications to the content of the

current course might be necessary. The delivery of the
course, however, would have to be altered significantly
to facilitate the simultaneous attendance of a large
number of managers from the same department. It would have
to be conducted over a period of weeks, in half-day or full-
day modules rather than over three straight days as at
present. Such an approach would minimise disruption to
normal work schedules and would facilitate the attendance
of managers who cannot or will not come to full-time courses.
It also has the advantage of allowing managers more time to
absorb large quantities of novel and complex information.
By focusing on all managers in a department, the course
militates against the tendency to think of information
technology as "someone else's responsibility - not mine" and
encourages managers, both individually and collectively, to
view the management of departmental information systems as
part of their general responsibilities.

Post-Foundation Course Development

It is clear that many aspects of information technology as
it relates to user managers cannot be covered adequately in
an introductory course, no matter how well it is organised.
A continuous programme of learning is required - the content
and depth of which depends very much on the nature of the
manager's work. For example, where the work is policy-
orientated, managers will wish to learn how to use
technology for planning and analysis, e.g., budgeting,
forecasting, comparing and contrasting, model-building, and
so on. A technology-orientated learning programme for such
managers would revolve around such topics as decision support
systems, the micro-computer as a management tool, evaluation
of various software packages, and defining information
requirements. Where the work is more administrative (e.g.,
claims processing) and where computer systems affect large

numbers of staff in key line divisions, managers will be
interested in a wider range of technology-related topics
(e.g., database, distributed data processing, systems
security, fraud control, and the ergonomics of workplace
design). Therefore they will need a longer and more
extensive programme of development than other managers.
However, three topics are likely to be of interest to all
managers: project management and control, strategic
planning and office automation. These are discussed in the
following appendices and a number of developmental
activities are suggested to help managers acquire a deeper
understanding of the isses raised in these important, but
complex areas.

APPENDIX C

Theme 2:   The Management and Control of Computer Projects

Project management is different from the management of
continuing functionally orientated work. Projects, by
definition, are single, non-repetitive enterprises. Project
management itself has been called the "business of securing
objectives in the face of all the risks and problems
encountered along the way."[1]

In the special context of computer projects, it is difficult
to separate the notion of project control per se from the
notion of systems development methodology. The two
concepts are becoming increasingly linked, particularly
as a result of the advent of database and structured methods
of systems development.

In the past, most authorities have tended to treat the
management of computer projects as comprising a clearly
defined set of techniques, all owing a great deal to
industrial project management. A typical introduction to
the subject identifies such elements as: defining
objectives and constraints, specifying stages, activities
and tasks, and monitoring progress.[2] Some reservations
have been expressed about the efficacy of such a simple
approach. Brooks, for example, cautions against an
overdependence on the analogy with industrial project
control:

---

[1] D. Lock, Project Management. Farnborough, Hants:
Gower Press, 1977, p.xi.

[2] Hoskyns Ltd., Project Management Course Notes –
Project Planning and Control Principles. John Hoskyns
& Co. Ltd., 91-3 Farringdon Road, London EC1, undated.

> In many ways, managing a large computer
> programming project is like managing any
> other large undertaking - in more ways than
> most programmers believe. But in many other
> ways it is different - in more ways than
> most professional managers expect.[1]

A small number of authors have remarked on the importance of human factors in the design of information systems.[2] An even smaller number have adopted a more holistic approach, derived from the important insights of cybernetics.[3]

The Importance of Project Management

Computer projects need to be planned and controlled carefully to avoid potential risks. The failure of a computer project could have a seriously damaging effect on the working of a department. Major projects involve a fundamental change in the way in which a department's work is carried out; they may require substantial resources and take years to complete. In some cases, previously untried hardware and software may be used. It may be difficult to insure against the risk of failure by making arrangements to return to a manual system should the project fall behind schedule. Often, the main reason for embarking on computerisation projects in the first place is that manual systems are breaking down. In these circumstances, a department cannot afford a project to fail. The purpose of project planning and control is to minimise the risk of

[1]   F.P. Brooks, The Mythical Man-Month. Reading, Mass.:
      Addison-Wesley, 1979, p.vii.

[2]   For example, E. Mumford and D. Hensall, A Participative
      Approach to Computer Systems Design. London:
      Associated Business Press, 1979.

[3]   The best example being R. Thomsett, People and Project
      Management. New York: Yourdon Press, 1980.

failure. Yet it has to be acknowledged that a large
proportion of past computer projects have been failures,
at least in the sense that target dates were missed and cost
budgets overrun. According to one writer, this has had the
result that:

> Many managements have become disillusioned
> with the inability of computer project
> leaders to meet targets of time and cost.
> However, the desire for better project
> control, when combined with the spurious
> idea that what is desirable is always
> possible, leads to the search for the
> "Holy Grail" - a method of control which
> will eliminate uncertainties. No such
> method exists.[1]

Synnott and Gruber identify four major contributing reasons
for this depressing state of affairs:

- project management is not an exact science
- cost estimates are generally made prematurely
- too many projects suffer from loose management
  control
- poor definition by the users results in bad
  specifications, leading to frequent requests for
  changes. [2]

Recent trends have tended to reinforce the need for
effective project control. There have been significant
moves away from centralised hardware to "distributed"
hardware. Increasingly, control of computer projects
is seen as the responsibility of user management rather
than of the technical specialists. Within the civil

---

[1] R. Wylie, Project Planning and Control for Data
     Processing. Manchester: National Computing Centre,
     1975, p.7.

[2] Synnott and Gruber, op. cit., p. 274.

service, there has been a trend towards the acquisition of packaged hardware and software solutions. This reduces the expensive and time-consuming process of building tailor-made systems, but it in no sense lessens the need for project management and control.

Approaches to Project Management and Control

A distinction has recently been drawn between the classic "phased" approach to project control and the newer "structured" approach.[1] The choice of these terms is not felicitious, since it is not being suggested that the phased approach is completely unstructured or that the structured approach does not include project phases. The classic "phased" approach derives primarily from the principles of scientific management put forward by F.W. Taylor and others in the early part of this century.[2] These principles maintain that:

- there is one best way of organising work
- most workers are like robots, needing only to be trained, motivated and supervised
- better tools and techniques are the prime means of improving productivity.

The main features of the classic approach are:

---

[1] For example, Thomsett, op. cit., who actually distinguishes three approaches: the classic phased approach, the improved phase approach and the structured approach.

[2] F.W. Taylor, The Principles of Scientific Management. New York: Harper & Row, 1911.

(i)   Divide the total project into phases. These
      phases are basically the same for all DP
      projects but there may be variations in
      individual cases (e.g., if a software
      package is purchased, the need for program
      specification, coding and testing may be
      eliminated). The outputs from each phase
      are fixed, normally as a formal document,
      and this represents a major decision point.

(ii) Estimate the resources required for each
      phase. Subdivide phases into smaller units
      and allocate resources accordingly.

(iii) Monitor progress against estimates using a
      formal reporting procedure. Act on progress
      reports as appropriate.

Critics of the classic approach argue that it is flawed in
that

- there is rarely one best way of organising work
- workers are complex and individualistic
- the prime means of increasing productivity are
  individual and group motivation.

This is not to suggest that the traditional phased
approach to systems development is worthless or irrelevant
- any standardised approach is likely to represent an
improvement over the absence of planning and control that
many observers say is characteristic of most DP projects.
Conventional applications development procedures are
accepted as being suitable in certain situations. For
example, James Martin, a leading computer expert, points
out that the classic approach is appropriate where user

requirements can be specified in fine detail before design and coding of a system begins.[1] Many computer systems in the civil service are of this type e.g., computerisation of taxation records. In these areas, standardised frameworks and guidelines have been developed that capitalise on accumulated experience, and within which there is ample scope for introducing improved methods and tools.

However, the number of computer applications where user requirements cannot be specified in detail in advance is increasing. In these instances, a more structured, user-driven approach to applications development is widely advocated. The structured approach encompasses a range of methods and techniques that have as a unifying feature an emphasis on producing documentation which can be reviewed by managers and users. This is in stark contrast to the classic phased approach, which tends to produce vast quantities of documentation that are incomprehensible to managers and users.

The main structured approach techniques are:

- structured analysis
- structured design
- structured programming
- top-down development
- programming teams
- structured walkthroughs.[2]

---

[1]   James Martin, Applications Development without Programmers. Englewood Cliffs, New Jersey: Prentice-Hall, Inc., 1981.

[2]   E. Yourdon, Managing the System Life Cycle. New York: Yourdon Press, 1982, pp.9-32.

A brief explanation of each of these techniques is given at
the end of this appendix.

The use of database software is often taken for granted in
the structured approach to applications development. This
would represent a significant step forward for the Irish
civil service, where the use of database is not widespread
outside the Office of the Revenue Commissioners. It is
important to emphasise that structured methods are not
simply technical tools that are of no concern to managers.
The main argument in favour of the use of structured
methods is that, for the first time, they render projects
manageable. According to Yourdon, structured methods
benefit managers and users because they

  - allow effective models of a system to be built in
    advance
  - ensure that the analysis, design and programming
    effort are visible
  - provide objective criteria for measuring quality
  - employ an interactive, top-down approach to building
    the system. [1]

Structured methods of systems development represent an
advance over the classic approach, but not a complete
revolution. Clearly there are elements of the phased
approach that remain valid for all types of computer
systems. These include activities such as:

  - project justification
  - estimating costs
  - progress recording
  - team-building and motivation.

---

[1] Yourdon, op. cit., p.7.

Proven techniques for many of these activities are well-known inside and outside the Irish civil service.

Delivery of Project Control Component

It has been argued that project management is unlike the day-to-day management of functionally orientated work. In contrast to strategic planning and office automation, project management is a subject to which formal classroom-based training can make a significant contribution. Many of the techniques that have been mentioned in the previous section can be covered in such a formal setting.

A distinction is often made between a loose assembly of methods and techniques and a fully fledged methodology. Many organisations promote packaged methodologies for systems development and project control and it would be possible to purchase and promote such a methodology for use within the Irish civil service. Dissemination of the standard methodology would than be the main purpose of this part of the development programme. There are some advantages in following this course: it would make for greater consistency between projects and would encourage standards of quality and control. However, there are important disadvantages associated with inflexible methodologies. Experience has shown that complicated and cumbersome systems cannot be enforced across a wide range of projects. Consequently, it is suggested that the emphasis should be on tried and tested methods rather than on elaborate methodologies.

Many commercial training organisations offer formal courses on project management. A brief analysis of the courses on offer in Ireland and Britain shows that most have failed to grasp the significance of improved methods of systems development and project management. No courses based on structured methods were found to be regularly offered in Ireland. Several organisations offer such courses in Britain including Jackson, Simpact, Structured Methods and Yourdon. Of these, Yourdon seems to support the widest range of courses and has the most impressive set of publications. However, the technical content of all these courses is high. They are more appropriate to organisation unit staff than senior user managers - the main target group of the proposed development programme. As was made clear in Appendix B, the roles and responsibilities of senior managers should be discussed initially in a foundation course and then explored later in special sessions.

The project control component of the proposed development programme should cover both the classic phased approach and the newer structured approach. The roles of the user and manager should be clearly defined and the critical importance of project justification, support, budgeting and testing of systems should be emphasised. In this way, the mistakes of earlier computer eras need not be repeated.

Brief Explanation of Main Structured Techniques

Structured analysis

This involves the use of graphic documentation tools to produce a functional system specification. These tools are

- data flow diagrams, which model the flow of data through a system
- data dictionary, which contains an organised collection of definitions of data items
- data structure diagrams, which describe the logical structure of complex files or data stores
- structured English, a subset of everyday English representing a compromise between the readability needed by users and the rigour needed by programmers.

Structured design

Structured design is an attempt to move away from the old cottage industry style of systems design towards a more disciplined style, with an emphasis on 'good' design. Good design is defined as cheap design - cheap to develop, cheap to operate and, above all, cheap to maintain.

Structured programming

Structured programming was the first of the structured techniques to gain widespread acceptance. It is now the norm rather than the exception.

Top-down development

Top-down development is a manifestation of the iterative project life cycle concept. It involves producing a prototype or skeleton version of the final system at an early stage, and thus allows the opportunity for users to verify that what they are going to get is what they really want.

Programming teams

Suggestions were made in the 1970s for improvements in the structure and composition of systems development teams. In particular, IBM embraced the concept of 'surgical' teams based on the practicality of the chief programmer team concept. Nevertheless, building teams and motivating staff remains one of the most important managerial functions.

Structured walkthroughs

The objective of each of the techniques of inspection, walkthrough and review is to detect and eliminate errors as early as possible in the system life cycle. In each case, formal roles are assigned to members of the review group and various reports are prescribed as outputs of the review session. The main difference between technical reviews and structured walkthroughs seems to be that the individual producer is not present at a review, but plays a major part in a walkthrough. It is now widely believed that both techniques are useful in reducing errors in systems.

APPENDIX D

Theme 3: Strategic Planning for Information Systems

The Concept of Strategic Planning

Strategic planning is distinct from operational planning,
project planning or budgeting techniques, which all are
inward-looking and are aimed at improving or controlling
established activities. [1]   By contrast, strategic
planning is outward-looking and future-orientated. It
involves anticipating, directing and controlling future
operations in pursuit of clearly defined objectives. The
development of long-term information technology plans is
part of this strategic planning process. Charting an
organisation's future course is uniquely a responsibility
for senior management; it is not a task to be delegated.
This is particularly so in the case of information
technology, where inadequate strategic planning can result
in mistakes which, if too expensive to rectify, will
severely constrain future choices and possibilities.

Need for Strategic Planning for Information Systems

Few Irish civil service departments have, as yet,
documented plans for information systems. Yet changing
circumstances in the civil service environment (e.g., the
trend away from centralised hardware and the growth in new
office technology) clearly point to the need for formal
planning within departments. Any technology-orientated
development programme for senior management, therefore,
must address the issue of strategic planning for information
technology. Without such a focus, there is a danger of
departments developing computer systems on a piecemeal,
project-by-project basis, resulting in inflexibile systems

---

[1]   Coopers & Lybrand Associates Ltd., Dublin, Deciding
      Information Strategy. Paper presented to the
      Department of the Environment, March 1983.

tied to incompatiable hardware. Such systems tend to be difficult and expensive to maintain and upgrade.

The problems of inflexible systems and incompatible hardware are likely to be even more pronounced in the office automation field than in traditional data processing. The question of planning for office automation is discussed at greater length in Appendix E. It will be argued that since computers and other forms of office equipment are tending to merge, it is necessary to take a broad view of information processing and to avoid planning for just the traditional areas of data processing. The view that strategic planning should form a major part of the proposed development programme was broadly confirmed both by senior specialist staff and by a number of line managers. In particular, it was pointed out that in the past the absence of strategic plans has led to some difficulties. For example, computer systems have often been developed only when manual systems were overloaded almost to the point of breakdown. In such situations, the planning phase was necessarily rushed and there was little time to investigate the broader, long-term consequences for the organisation of the proposed computer system.

Further confirmation of the importance of strategic planning for information systems is implied by the view that information should be regarded as an organisational resource. This view, which has gained considerable popularity in recent years, suggests that information should be managed as a resource, in much the same way as personnel, finance and materials are managed as resources. [1] If this view is accepted, then the real challenge of the new information

---

[1] J. Diebold, Forward to the Diebold Group Special Report, Information Resource Management: New Directions in Management, Infosystems, October 1979.

technologies for "information-intensive" organisations,
like government departments, lies not in technology but in
information. Information exists in many forms, e.g., data
(staff numbers, wage rates), text (letters, reports), image
(graphs, charts) and voice (meetings, telephone
conversations) and can be stored, processed and/or
communicated. In planning for computer-based information
systems, senior management in the civil service will have
to consider current and future information requirements -
in what form, for what purpose and to whom certain kinds
of information should be available. Otherwise, there is a
danger of the tail wagging the dog, of solutions chasing
problems, of technology being applied for its own sake
rather than as a considered answer to a defined
organisational need or problem.

Policy Issues and Methodologies

It would be misleading to regard strategic planning as a
straightforward technique or set of techniques. Drucker
points out that it

> ...is not a box of tricks, a bundle of techniques...
> some of the most important questions in strategic
> planning can be phrased only in terms such as "larger"
> or "smaller", "sooner" or "later". These terms cannot
> easily be manipulated by quantitative techniques. And
> some equally important areas: such as those of
> political climate, social responsibilities or human
> (including managerial) resources, cannot be quantified
> at all... strategic planning is not "the application
> of scientific methods to business decisions". It is
> the application of thought, analysis, imagination and
> judgement. It is responsibility rather than
> techniques. [1]

---

[1] Peter Drucker, Management: Tasks, Responsibilities,
    Practices. London: Pan Books, 1979.

From this point of view, any attempt to reduce strategic planning to a simple methodology loses sight of the essential nature of the strategic planning process.

It is possible to look outside the civil service for guidelines on strategic planning, but it would be wrong to place undue reliance on external sources. Most of the published material relating to strategic planning for information systems is concerned with private industry. In drawing up strategic plans for information systems, departments will have to take account of a number of policy issues that are irrelevant to most private organisations. In particular, they will have to consider:

- the degree to which the department will be reliant for computer services on the Central Computing Service (CCS) or on any other computer bureau

- the need for developments in computerisation to be coordinated throughout the civil service, i.e., the fact that departmental plans will have to be reviewed centrally to ensure compatibility and adherence to various centrally-defined technical standards

- the need to comply with the terms of any new technology agreements negotiated between the DPS and staff associations/trade unions.

These broad policy issues will form the background against which departmental plans will be set. However, the major policy issue facing departments will be the development of their own information policy. Such a policy would address the following issues:

- the relevance of information systems to departmental objectives

- the extent of integration of information systems within the department

- communication with other departments and agencies and with the public

- the present and future penetration of information technology

- data privacy and security policy.

Very few organisations have published their information policies. Yet Britain's Department of Health and Social Security (DHSS) is said to be moving towards the "whole-person concept". In the long run, this implies that full details of a person's dealings with the DHSS would be available at a terminal in every local office, rather than being held by a multiplicity of agencies at widely dispersed locations. This could be seen as an example of the sort of issue which needs to be settled by a departmental information policy. It exemplifies the whole question of "stand alone" systems versus "integrated" systems. Stand-alone systems are appropriate in circumstances in which data used by one system are rarely required by another. Conversely, an integrated system approach is appropriate where there are complex inter-relationships between systems. In many cases this will suggest that database software be used. Database can offer substantial benefits to the user, particularly in reducing the duplication or redundancy of data. However, to install database requires a significant investment in hardware, software and training, and this involves an important policy decision, which has to be made early in the development of strategic plans.

The diagnostic stage in strategic planning is the most important and most difficult. Once the key issues influencing future strategy have been identified and the

critical factors affecting the need for information systems
have been analysed, the actual process of drawing up plans
is comparatively straightforward. A number of formal
methodologies exist to help produce the plans. Although
there are differences between methodologies, most involve
a staged approach to planning:

The first stage generally involves a review of the
department's objectives in relation to information
systems.

The second stage is concerned with a review of the
current status of computerisation within the department.
In particular, it is necessary to review each
application currently being processed by computer in
terms of objectives, hardware and software
implications, costs and benefits, user acceptance,
standards, security, and its potential for further
development.

The third stage is to identify major new areas for the
development of computer applications. Some of the
specific topics to be addressed are:

  - scope for benefits and likely costs
  - resource requirements
  - hardware and software implications
  - staffing implications
  - management implications
  - risk assessment.

At this point, the aim is to produce a portfolio
of potential systems described at a functional or
logical level.

Having reviewed the development options, the fourth and
final stage is the production of the plans themselves.
These will outline the priorities for development and
will include a financial justification, a resources plan
and an implementation schedule. Obviously, annual plans
will be at a more detailed level than five-year plans,
but the broad structure will be similiar. Five-year
plans are normally rolled forward, with a major
review every two or three years.

Delivery of the Strategic Planning Component

Strategic planning for departmental information systems is
clearly an important topic for user managers and should
be addressed in any technology-orientated development
programme. In essence, it involves two aspects:

- The identification and analysis of policy issues,
  e.g., the relationship between the department and
  central services, deparmental information policies,
  new technology agreements

- The formulation and production of strategic plans.

Neither of these areas can be taught, since any discussion
on strategic planning for departmental information systems
must be set firmly in the organisational and social context
of the entire civil service and the particular government
department. Although the civil service will naturally take
cognizance of general developments in information technology,
there will be only limited scope for the direct participation
of outside agencies in any discussion of major policy
issues. These will be and should be settled within the
civil service itself.

However, there may be some opportunity for consulting expert opinion. This is broadly the approach adopted by the Civil Service College in Britain. In conjunction with the Central Computer and Telecommunications Agency and the London Business School, the College has sponsored a three-day course entitled 'Top Management and the Information Resource: The Challenge of the New Technology'. It is designed for audiences drawn equally from the public and private sectors. The course identifies the substantive issues and policy options associated with information resources; establishes the need for a positive approach by top management to the formulation of an information policy; identifies current technological developments; and examines their implications. It takes account of the organisational and social impact of the new technology and examines the question of getting value for money. It would not be difficult to organise a similar course for senior civil servants in Ireland. Inviting representatives from the private sector might be thought to be desirable. An exercise of this nature could play an important part in bringing the issues into the open. However, it would not be a substitute for the complex and difficult process of formulating and disseminating clear policies.

Regarding the task of producing strategic plans, several commercial organisations offer formal courses on the process of strategic planning for information systems. Since these courses are geared towards private sector organisations, they are unlikely to meet fully the needs of the civil service. A more productive approach would be the organisation of a series of workshops involving DPS/CCS representatives and senior departmental managers; these

could be both service-wide and departmentally based. Where
appropriate, outside authorities could be invited to
contribute to the workshops.

Inter-departmental liaison groups could be formed (most
likely comprising senior departmental organisation and
planning unit staff); these officers would meet from
time to time to discuss strategic planning issues. The
feasibility of forming such inter-departmental liaison
groups at top management level (i.e., Assistant Secretary/
Secretary) should also be considered. In summary, we
recommend that the following activities be undertaken to
increase senior managers' understanding of strategic
planning for information systems:

   (i)   Briefing by experts and policy workshops/
         seminars

  (ii)   Workshops on the process of strategic planning
         and the steps involved in producing plans - both
         service-wide and departmentally based

 (iii)   The formation of inter-departmental liaison
         groups at (a) top management level and (b) senior
         organisation/planning unit level.

APPENDIX E

Theme 4: Office Automation and Other
"New" Technology Applications

The Challenge of Office Automation

Office automation has been defined as "people using technology to manage and communicate information more effectively." [1] Unlike traditional data processing, which deals with the formal side of information handling and works to a set of well-defined rules for each application (e.g., payroll, accounts), office automation focuses on the more undefined, less structured aspects of an organisation's total information system (e.g., document preparation, message distribution, personal information management and information access). [2] Proportionately more white-collar workers are involved in these less well-defined activities than in routine data processing. To computerise these systems, therefore, poses greater challenges for organisations than traditional DP. The jobs of many more people will be affected, up to and including senior management. Consequently, organisational structures and procedures, established job practices and responsibilities, career systems, pay policy and many other aspects of organisational functioning may have to be modified to accommodate new systems of working. The changes will have to be negotiated and the adoption of new office technology is likely to be evolutionary rather than revolutionary. Such is the case already in the Irish civil service, where new office facilities (principally word processing) are being introduced slowly but surely. Most authorities believe that office automation will be a major concern for public service organisations in the 1980s and 1990s. As Barron and Curnow maintain:

[1] Department of the Public Service, Office Automation in the Civil Service: What Managers Need to know. Computer exhibition leaflet, 1984.

[2] S.G. Price, Introducing the Electronic Office. Manchester: National Computing Centre, 1979, p.12.

> In the long term, the development of electronic
> information will have greater implications for
> Government than for any other part of the economy,
> since a vast part of government apparatus is
> concerned with the acquisition and dissemination
> of information. [1]

It is impossible to predict what these implications will be
for particular public service organisations. Technology is
a tool, not a determinant. It is a force for change but
does not in itself determine the nature and magnitude of
that change. Changes are the result of managerial choice
and will differ from one organisation to another, even
where identical systems are installed. Office automation
clearly poses a challenge for management and staff; it
should not be seen as a threat to the whole structure of
the civil service.

Main Components of Office Automation

Office automation is an umbrella term covering the use of
a variety of technologies to handle information in the
office. Most of the familiar items of office equipment in
use today were developed in the last century: the
telephone, the typewriter, the adding machine and the
duplicator are all nineteenth-century machines. They have
been modified and improved upon gradually. However, in the
last ten years two developments have revolutionised office
equipment: the advent of the microprocessor and improvements
in telecommunications.

---

[1] I. Barron and R. Curnow, The Future with
    Microelectronics. Milton Keynes: Open University
    Press, 1979, p.216

The incorporation of microprocessors and communications
facilities has led to dramatic improvements in the
usefulness of familiar items of equipment. However, the
most important single trend has been the convergence of
computers, office equipment and telecommunications.

The automated office or "office of the future" is based on
the convergence of these technologies. It will soon be
possible to have a single multi-purpose workstation on
every desk, to replace the variety of machines used
currently (e.g., telephone, calculator, typewriter,
photocopier). Such a workstation would resemble today's
computer terminal, but would have much wider functions.
Using such a workstation, it would be possible to:

   - generate and amend texts
   - send and receive massages
   - retrieve information from local and remote sources
   - carry out data processing functions
   - perform calculations, draw graphs, and so on

Some commentators believe that today's personal computer
will be the workstation of tomorrow, particularly for
managerial and professional staff. In the words of one
writer: "The long-sought multi-function office workstation
has arrived, disguised as the personal computer."[1]
Although a major weakness of the personal computer is its
lack of communication facilities (the majority are stand-
alone machines) an increasing percentage (estimated at
between 20% and 30% in the US) are being connected to
larger computers or "networked" to other microcomputers,

[1] R.R. Aranda, Personal Computers as Workstations.
    Proceedings of the Digital Equipment Users Society,
    St. Louis, Missouri, May 1983, p.169.

giving the user access to databases, electronic mail and
to advanced electronic filing facilities. Future
developments are likely to include speech recognition
and expert systems to help with decision-making - concepts
that are central to the Japanese proposals for fifth-
generation computers.[1]

Almost all the facilities that will be in the workstation
of the future are already available in various forms.
Figure 3 overleaf traces the development paths of the
various strands that comprise the new technology in
relation to seven major areas of office administration:[2]

Data processing:	manipulation of structured information
Text processing:	manipulation of information in the form of written words
Image processing:	processing of visual information
Voice processing:	information in the form of spoken words
Communication:	transferring information from one point to another
Storage and retrieval:	storing and retrieving information in any form
Decision-making:	making judgments on the basis of information.

[1] Japanese Information Processing Development Centre
    (JIPDC), Preliminary Report on Study and Research of
    Fifth Generation Computers. JIPDC, 1981.

[2] This classification is a revised and expanded version
    of that given in D.W. Birchall & V.J. Hammond,
    Tomorrow's Office Today. London: Business Books,
    1981, p.14.

Figure 3: Developments in the Field of Office Automation

INFORMATION – RELATED FUNCTIONS	TECHNOLOGIES				
Data processing	Calculators, Accounting machines	Batch computers, Interactive computers	Personal computers		
Text processing	Typewriters, Electronic typewriters	Stand-alone wordprocessors	Shared logic wordprocessors	Voice input	
Image processing	Pencil and paper, Duplicators	Intelligent copiers, Facsimile	Computer graphics	Video disc	
Voice processing	Dictation, Dictation machines, Answering machines	Private Automatic Branch Exchanges (PABX)	Computer voice recognition		
Communications	Mail, Telephone, Telex	Computer networks	Packet-switched systems (PSS), Teletex	Electronic mail, Teleconferencing	Local/wide area networks
Storage and retrieval	Paper, Reference books	Micrographics	Videotex, Database, Electronic filing	Bubble memory	
Decision-making	Management information systems (MIS)	Financial modelling	Expert systems		

'THE ELECTRONIC OFFICE'

The early technologies applied to these functions are listed
listed on the left-hand side of the diagram. Technologies
represented in the middle range include many currently
employed in the Irish civil service. Advanced technologies,
represented on the right-hand side of the figure, although
not yet widely available, are all being developed. A
brief account of current trends in the development of
these technologies is given in the following pages.

Data Processing

Computers have been used for data processing in the civil
service for many years. Traditionally, the emphasis has
been on centralised batch processing with a limited on-
line service. Recently the trend has been towards the
installation of minicomputers with interactive
capabilities. In the past, the emphasis has also been on
processing individual transactions of a routine nature
(e.g., social welfare claims), but some progress has been
made in providing management information, e.g., analysis
of trends, breakdown of expenditure by group, geographical
area, and so on.

Text Processing

Stand-alone word processors became widely available in the
mid-1970s. It was then possible to install a machine on
which a text could be written and edited much more
efficiently than on a typewriter. Increased productivity
of over 100% was frequently reported.[1] In the late 1970s,
shared logic systems were introduced which enabled word
processing terminals to share printers and disc drives,
thus reducing costs still further. Some progress has also

[1] Price, op. cit., p.244.

been made on direct voice input to computers and word processing systems. NEC of Japan has released a speech recogniser with a vocabulary of 500 words; it is used by the Japanese postal service for parcel sorting.[1] More ambitiously, the research goals of the Japanese Fifth Generation project include the development of a phonetic typewriter that is capable of sentence construction; it will be able to recognise 10,000 spoken words. By the end of the 1980s, when this stage is reached, text and voice processing will effectively have converged.

Image Processing

The processing of pictorial information has been improved by better photocopying and facsimile transmission. When communicating word processors become widespread, it is likely that much paper-based correspondence will be dispensed with altogether. Documents will be transmitted from the originator's screen to the recipient's and will be printed only if the recipient requires a paper or "hard" copy. Another important development has been the introduction of computer graphics packages that allow complex data (in the form of numbers and words) to be represented visually.

Voice Processing

Communication through the spoken work is probably the most important means of exchanging information in any organisation. Advanced voice-handling facilities are now available: the microprocessor-based Private Automatic Branch Exchanges (PABX) These include:

---

[1] Computing, March 4 1982.

            call redirection
            automatic call back
            conference calls
            abbreviated number dialling
            call-logging
            voice store and forward.

As the telecommunications network adopts digital technology,
the distinction between voice and data communications will
become increasingly blurred.

Communications

Substantial sums are being invested in the
telecommunications system: the new public packet-switched
system (PSS), being installed by Telecom Eireann, will be
cheaper to use than the existing telephone system. This
will make teleprocessing more attractive.

For many organisations, the first step into office
automation will be TELETEX - a worldwide text
communication system replacing TELEX. At the same time,
electronic mail systems are being developed. Electronic
mail is a development of the store and forward concept,
whereby messages are delivered to the recipient's
electronic mailbox. An experimental electronic mail
service was installed within the Department of Posts
and Telegrpahs in 1982. As the system expands, businesses
may be expected to switch from ordinary postal delivery
to electronic mail to a significant extent, since
electronic mail is less expensive.

One of the most pervasive influences in bringing together
elements of technology has been the development of local
area networks. Using a local network, it is possible to

link mainframe and microcomputers, computer peripherals, telephone handsets and PABXs. The network itself consists of a loop of twisted wire or coaxial cable installed in the department or section, with standard sockets at convenient locations. The main advantage of a network is that it allows cheap communication and the efficient sharing of expensive resources such as computer peripherals. It is cheaper to install than a centralised mainframe computer system of equivalent power and is also much less expensive to upgrade. Terminals on the local network can be used for data processing, word processing, electronic mail, electronic filing, or whatever.

Storage and Retrieval

Traditionally, paper has been the primary medium for information storage. For long-term archival storage, however, micrographics offer an attractive alternative. Some applications in the civil service already use computer output microfilm (COM). Database techniques are also being adopted. The use of a computer database within a department or section can be regarded as a means of reducing the duplication or redundancy of data, which occurs when each application keeps its own data files. If information is a resource, a database system can be seen as a tool for managing that resource more efficiently.

Departments may also be interested in access to public (as opposed to departmental) databases. One easy means of gaining access to a remote database is provided by videotex. Videotex systems include Viewdata, which is provided by P & T authorities, and Teletext, which is provided by broadcasting authorities. Both services can be received via modified television sets.

Decision-Making

At present, most computer systems in the civil service are
geared towards the processing of routine transactions. The
use of computers in decision-making is currently quite
limited, primarily because the information needed to create
decision-making models for planning and budgetary purposes
is either not available or exists in a relatively
inaccessible form. However, many government departments
and agencies are currently developing microcomputer-based
financial modelling systems - an area of application in
which there is a large selection of comparatively cheap
software packages. Larger and more complex decision-
making models are being developed in the Departments of
Health and Social Welfare, where serious attempts are being
made to create departmental databases which can be used for
a wide variety of planning, budgetary and management
information purposes.

A different and somewhat more arcane use of computers in
decision-making are so-called "expert systems", which are
used by professionals, mostly in medicine and engineering.
At present, there are reported to be over 40 expert systems
throughout the world and the first general purpose packages
are now becoming available.[1] As the variety of expert
systems increases and departments become more
technologically advanced, they will no doubt explore
the potential of these systems for their professional and
technical staff.

---

[1] Computer Talk, March 22 1982.

Planning for Office Automation

The introduction of office automation is perhaps best seen as a process, not a project. Unlike most data processing applications, which can be regarded as finite projects, office automation applications involve a long-term process with wide-ranging implications. In the long run, the objective is to integrate a range of information processing functions. This objective could be thwarted if incompatible hardware is bought and installed. This poses a serious problem. Price notes that:

> A shortage of standards in the electronic area is likely to act as a major hindrance to its development.[1]

He suggests that standards are required for telecommunications, the interchange of media, operator interfaces and data representation. Unfortunately, the present position is far from satisfactory, partly because manufacturers of office automation equipment have widely differing backgrounds - mainframe and mini-computers, typewriters, copiers, communications devices, semiconductors, and so on. With the myriad of suppliers on the market, it is easy to buy incompatible equipment. As a result, operator training costs are increased, one machine cannot be used to back up another, and the possibility of linking word processors in the future is reduced substantially. Within the civil service, it is important that policy decisions are taken to minimise the problems of incompatibility in the office automation field. It may be necessary to restrict purchases to a relatively small number of manufacturers and ranges of equipment, as had already happened in the health services. Even though the general trend in office systems is towards

---

[1] Price, op. cit., p.90.

convergence, it should not be assumed that this will happen
without planning and effort.

Birchall and Hammond offer some general advice on how to
plan for office automation.[1] The first step is to
review the organisation's present stage of development –
the type of equipment used and the numbers employed,
communications patterns and loadings, and how the
information requirements are being met. The second step
is to examine communications and information processing
in its broadest context, so that equipment can be chosen
for the long term. Changes in staffing requirements and
types of skill required should be anticipated.

Synnott and Gruber offer rather more detailed advice, based
on the assumption that office automation evolves through
four stages:[2]

Initiation   – mechanical efficiency primarily
through wordprocessing

Expansion   – the rapid introduction of new
tools, such as electronic mail and
filing

Formalisation   – the proliferation of office
systems, and the greater need for
integration

Maturity   – integration into a cohesive office
system; shifting the emphasis from
mechanising tasks to automating
functions.

---

[1] Birchall and Hammond, op. cit., p.12.

[2] Synnott and Gruber, op. cit., p.263.

Accordingly, planning for office automation should follow
a four-phase process.

Phased Office Information Systems Strategy

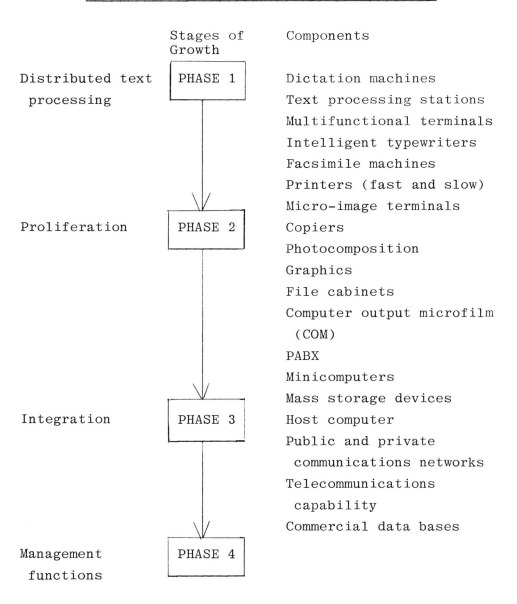

Stages of Growth		Components
Distributed text processing	PHASE 1	Dictation machines
		Text processing stations
		Multifunctional terminals
		Intelligent typewriters
		Facsimile machines
		Printers (fast and slow)
		Micro-image terminals
Proliferation	PHASE 2	Copiers
		Photocomposition
		Graphics
		File cabinets
		Computer output microfilm (COM)
		PABX
		Minicomputers
		Mass storage devices
Integration	PHASE 3	Host computer
		Public and private communications networks
		Telecommunications capability
		Commercial data bases
Management functions	PHASE 4	

The list of components given by Synnott and Gruber is
rather eccentric. In phase one, the objective should be
to introduce new technology, primarily for text processing,
without disturbing the organisation's structure. Thus
they warn against the outdated strategy of creating a
centralised typing pool. They also suggest starting with
a "friendly" application on a pilot basis.

In phase two, office components, such as paper and filing
cabinets, begin to be replaced as extra capabilities are
added gradually to the text processing function.

In phase three, the emphasis in on creating a single
integrated system using multi-purpose workstations.

The final stage involves the automation of management
functions, as opposed to clerical tasks. This will depend
on the introduction of management workstations, which
will not require specialised knowledge or training to use.
Synnott and Gruber argue that these stages must be
followed in the order given because each stage builds on
the one before.

Two important points emerge from most discussions of
planning for office automation. The first is that the
techniques of systems analysis and design used in data
processing are inadequate for the introduction of
automated office services.[1] Changes in office
procedures require a broad understanding of behavioural
factors. Many observers note that human considerations
are of paramount importance. Office automation will have
more significant long-term implications for the organisation
of the civil service than data processing. This implies

[1] Central Computer and Telecommunications Agency
    (CCTA), New Office Technology in the Civil Service.
    London: CCTA, 1980.

that office automation poses more management problems than technical problems.

The second important point is that there are benefits to be gained from setting up pilot projects in controlled situations. Here, there are lessons to be learned from the CCTA office technology exploratory programme in Britain where pilot projects ran into technical and non-technical problems that might have been foreseen. [1]

Delivery of the Office Automation Component

We have identified three aspects of office automation which should be included in the proposed technology-orientated development programme for senior managers in the civil service:

> Awareness courses
> Planning for office automation
> Pilot projects.

Each of these should be approached differently. As a first step, users must be given the proper background 'awareness' information. This is the approach adopted by Civil Service College in Britain, which sponsored a series of seminars on "Information Technology and the Civil Service". Most introductory computer appreciation courses (including those developed by the Civil Service Training Centre) include an element on office technology. Where these are supplemented by "hands-on" experience, such courses offer a useful introduction to office automation.

[1]   Central Computer and Telecommunications Agency (CCTA), Early Experience with Multi-User Office Systems (IT series No.7). London: HMSO (CCTA), April 1984.

It would be unrealistic, however, to attach too much importance to formal courses. More important from a managerial point of view would be a series of discussions on the issues relating to planning for the onset of office automation. There would be some scope here for briefings by experts. Site visits to organisations that have made progress in office automation would also be helpful. But perhaps the most important step forward would be to mount a series of carefully chosen and managed pilot projects in the civil service. The experience of the British office automation pilot programme indicates that pilot projects should ideally

- employ proven technology, thus minimising the risk of failure because of hardware or software inadequacies

- be sited in typical offices

- be supported by management and staff at all levels

- be directed at areas of direct public benefit, and not just to achieve administrative efficiency

- be managed by a project team with an all-round grasp of the human, technological and project management aspects of systems design.

Now would be an excellent time to start on a programme of pilot projects, for several reasons. First, many technologies have reached the point where they are clearly cost-justified. Data and wordprocessing technologies are the most obvious examples, but graphics, electronic mail, electronic filing and videotex systems are also economic possibilities. Secondly, it is clear that

organisations have to climb a "learning curve" as they
introduce new technology; a small investment at an early
stage pays significant dividends. Third, and perhaps
most important, substantial progress has been made towards
providing a nationwide digital communications network,
using microwave technology.

APPENDIX F

Invitation to Form a Management
Information Technology Learning Group in
the Department of Social Welfare

<u>INVITATION TO FORM A SENIOR MANAGEMENT INFORMATION</u>
<u>TECHNOLOGY LEARNING GROUP IN THE DEPARTMENT OF SOCIAL</u>
<u>WELFARE</u>

The Department of Social Welfare has accepted an
invitation to participate in a technology-orientated
management development programme. The need for such
a programme was identified by a DPS-commissioned
research project undertaken by the IPA. We hope
that you, as a senior departmental manager, will
agree to participate in the learning programme, which
we hope will benefit you personally as well as your
organisation as a whole. The following is a brief
outline of why such a programme is necessary, and the
approach we intend to take in relation to the
Management Information Technology (MIT) Group.

<u>Background</u>

The trend towards decentralisation of computer
facilities in the civil service, and the consequent
devolution of accountability and responsibility, will
lead to a greater awareness in departments of the
potential of computers. To date, to a great extent,
computers have been looked upon as "beasts of burden",
machines to do the routine work, and have been under-
utilised in generating information and statistics for
use by management in decision-making and policy
development.

Management systems and office automation both
require more active and extensive user management
involvement than traditional data processing systems.
To make the best use of these new information
technologies, senior managers in this Department and

other Government departments will require new
knowledge and skills, both to control and manage
individual computer projects and to contribute
effectively to the development of departmental plans
in relation to the use of information technology.

Management IT Group

We propose to base the MIT Group on the principles of
action learning, i.e., learning by doing, both
individually and in a group. Experience with this
technique in other countries has shown that it works
best when members work on a project of practical
significance and direct relevance to their own work
situation. The existence of several on-going projects
in the Department of Social Welfare makes the
Department an ideal location to try out such a
strategy.

It is also known that maximum benefit is derived from
this learning-by-doing process if it takes place in
the company of others who are undergoing a similar
experience and it is preferable that members be
drawn from the same managerial strata in the
organisation. This is why we will be concentrating
on managers at Assistant Principal and Principal level.
Members of the MIT group will meet at regular
intervals (say once or twice a month) to discuss
their learning requirements and to decide on
appropriate learning activities.

The subject areas that the management group are likely
to want to concentrate upon are:

    1. The general topic of information technology;

concepts, uses and organisational
implications

2. Managing and controlling computerisation
   projects

3. Strategic planning for the Department's
   information systems

4. Office automation.

Group members will be supported by an experienced
group facilitator/trainer, who will help the group
clarify its learning needs in relation to these areas,
and help them monitor the extent to which the needs so
identified are actually met in practice. Mary Rose
Greville, head of the IPA Management Programme, will
fill this role, advised by Evelyn Blennerhassett, the
Institute's principal researcher in the personnel/
human resources management area. Vera Dervan of the
Department's Computer Operations and Development Unit
will act as liaison between the IPA and the Department.

Proposed Programme Is Different

The proposed technology-orientated development
programme differs from management training as usually
understood in several important respects:

-   It focuses on the specific needs of one
    department in a particular area - technology -
    rather than the broad general management
    development needs of the civil service as a
    whole.

- It is both group-orientated and individual-
  orientated. The emphasis is on developing
  managers at senior level capable of
  understanding and managing technology.

- A broad mix of learning activities is provided,
  some classroom-based, others action-based.

- As far as possible all learning experiences are
  held in-house i.e., within the physical
  confines of the Department itself. Experts are
  brought to the organisation, rather than vice
  versa.

- The emphasis is on learning rather than
  training, managers taking responsibility for
  their own development rather than relying on
  others to tell them what they should know.
  Active rather than passive learning is
  encouraged. With the help of a facilitator,
  managers will learn to define their own needs
  as well as the general developmental needs of
  the management group as a whole.

To the best of our knowledge, such a management
development programme has never been undertaken in a
Government department in Ireland.

The results of the proposed programme in the
Department of Social Welfare will be written up in the
form of a research report by the IPA - a report which
it is hoped will benefit other departments interested
in undertaking a similar programme.

Depending on the management group's wishes, some or
all of the following learning events could form
part of the proposed development programme:

1. An introductory course for those with only
    a limited knowledge of technology and its
    implications

2. Problem-solving sessions where the group
    tackles current problems

3. Special assignments for one or more members
    of the group

4. Briefings by experts on particular topics and
    by one member of the group to others. (The
    IT group will include management analysts,
    computer specialists as well as user
    managers)

5. Vendors' demonstrations and site visits both
    within the Department and to other
    organisations, to view other systems

6. In-house workshops on particular topics

7. Individual or group study programmes using
    video-based training materials which can be
    used in-house and assimilated by the learner
    at his or her own pace

8. The formation of inter-departmental user
    groups to facilitate the exchange of
    information, ideas and experience

9. The setting up of a technology-orientated
    departmental library.

It will not be necessary for group members
participate in all learning activities. He or she
may choose those which best suit their needs. The
essence of the development programme is that it
should be pertinent to the manager's own concerns.

APPENDIX G

Pre-Programme Computer Literacy Test for MIT Group Members

In relation to each of the following information technology concepts or terms, how would you describe your current level of knolwedge or understanding?

For each item, please choose a number based on the following scale:

1 = Absolutely no knowledge/understanding - have never even heard the term

2 = Almost no knowledge/understanding - have heard the term but would not be able to explain it to someone else

3 = A little knowledge/understanding - could, if pressed, make a stab at explaining it to someone else

4 = A moderate knowledge/understanding - could give a reasonably good layman's explanation to someone else

5 = A good knowledge/understanding - would feel confident if asked to explain it to someone else

Batch processing _____	Mainframes, minis and _____ micros: their pros and cons
	Data carriers _____
Transaction processing _____	Database _____
	Testing, e.g., systems _____ program, acceptarce
Distributed processing _____	Fallback arrangements _____
	Control reporting _____
High-and low-level _____ languages	Post-implementation _____ maintenance
	Configuration _____

Systems software	——	Applications software	——	Daisy Wheel
Turnkey packages	——	Hardward convergence	——	Expert systems
Structured files	——	Time-sharing	——	Interactive system
On-line systems	——	Real time systems	——	Optical character reading
Peripherals	——	Menu-driven language	——	Workstation
File creation	——	File conversion	——	CPU
Network	——	DIANE	——	Shared logic

APPENDIX   H

Summary of MIT Group Learning Activities

SUMMARY OF MIT GROUP LEARNING ACTIVITIES

Month	Topic Covered	Presentation Details
December '83	Launch of MIT Group	First meeting of MIT Group. Development programme launched officially by Assistant Secretary (Computer Operations & Development), who stressed the importance of information technology to the Department's operations and the need for good management and effective planning to make the best use of technology. Current and future problems and challenges were outlined and top management's support was expressed for the MIT group initiative. Half-day session.
January '84	Foundation Course: Part 1	Introduction to basic computer concepts and methods of data processing, followed by a visit to the computer room and a demonstration of the Department's National Enquiry System. Presentation by senior CDPS manager and DSW organisation unit/computer development staff. Group discussion. Half-day session.
	Foundation Course: Part 2	Presentation by DSW organisation/unit/ computer development staff, outlining

Month	Topic Covered	Presentation Details
February '84		current and future systems in the Department. Further clarification of systems development cycle and software concepts by CDPS manager. Group discussion. Half-day session.
	Agreeing Draft Programme	Clarification of individual and group learning needs. Draft programme decided, based on managers' own suggestions and input from the researcher. Half-day session.
	Word Processing	Site visit by MIT group to Civil Service Commission (CSC) to see word processing in action. Presentation and real-life demonstration of word processing and list
	List Processing	processing by CSC manager, followed by
	Optical Mark Reading (OMR)	demonstration of optical mark reading (OMR). A second site visit was organised in May '84 for MIT members unable to attend in February. Half-day session.
	Decision Support Models	Demonstration by MIT **group** manager of decision support models developed on a microcomputer in the Department. First introduction to concept of computer as a management tool for use in decision-making

Month	Topic Covered	Presentation Details
		and financial control activities. Half-day session.
	Computers in Personnel	Attendance by one MIT group member at seminar by Telecom Eireann in Civil Service Training Centre, on issues and problems encountered in designing a computerised personnel system for 18,000 employees. Evening seminar.
March '84	Office Automation	Seminar organised by Digital Ireland. Presentations by a number of speakers, followed by visit to DECTOWN to see how office automation facilities might be used in different managerial areas, e.g., accounts, personnel. Full day session.
	Review Session	Review of value and usefulness of recent learning activities. Half-day session.
	Information Technology in the Civil Service	Attendance by one MIT group member at CSTC 3-day course on information technology and the civil service, incorporating "hands-on" experience at a microcomputer.

Month	Topic Covered	Presentation Details
March '84	Technology and Trainers	Attendance by one MIT group member at 1½-day North-South Trainers' Conference in Institute of Public Administration.
	Database: Concept and Strategy	Half-day session on database, using commercial video training package, with CDPS content expert as group discussion leader.
	Distributed Data Processing	Half-day session on distributed data processing, using commercial video training package, with CDPS content expert as group discussion leader. Informal talk by DSW computer operations manager on communications, technology and the Department.
	COMPUTEX and CSTC Exhibitions	Attendance by some MIT group members at major COMPUTEX exhibition in RDS and CTSC-sponsored exhibition in Mansion House.

Month	Topic Covered	Presentation Details
April '84	An Post and DSW: Electronic Funds Transfer	Presentation by Head of Retail/Banking, An Post, on current and future facilities. Discussion of such topics as electronic funds transfer, smart card technology, plastic card technology, and how such developments might be useful for the Department of Social Welfare. Half-day session.
	Review Session	Review of value and usefulness of recent learning activities.
	Integrating Office Automation and Data Processing	Half-day session on integrating office automation and data processing in the work environment, using commercial video training package, with CDPS content expert as group discussion leader. Outline by another CDPS manager of possible office automation pilots in DSW.
May '84	Decision Support Systems	Seminar by commercial consultancy organisation on decision support systems

Month	Topic Covered	Presentation Details
May '84		and management. Examples from the British civil service and demonstration of software, using data supplied by MIT group member. Half-day session.
	Management Information System in Department of Health	Visit by some MIT group members to Department of Health, to discuss that department's approach to and progress on the development of a departmental information system. Half-day session.
	"People" Issues in Computerisation	Presentation by one MIT group member on the human side of technology, how to avoid "people" problems. Group discussion. Half-day session.
	Developing a Management Information Service for the Department of Social Welfare	Presentation by two MIT group members on current position regarding management information in the Department, and proposal for the development of a Management Information Service to meet management's needs. Group discussion of possible

Month	Topic Covered	Presentation Details
		approaches. Commitment by MIT group to actively support this initiative and report on its success. Half-day session.
	Problems Encountered in Managing the Information Resource	Presentation by management services professional from Guinness Ireland on problems, issues and strategies associated with the management and control of information. Group discussion on relevance to Department of Social Welfare. Half-day session.
June '84	Computer-aided Method for Describing Systems (CAMDAS)	Visit to Irish Life Assurance Co. by some MIT group members to test the relevance and ease of use of an Irish Life software package for describing and automating systems. A specific functional area of the Department's activities was modelled for the purpose of the demonstration and test. Half-day session. Further half-day follow-up session held in October '84.

Month	Topic Covered	Presentation Details
	Computer Security and Fraud Control	Session on methods for ensuring security of computer systems and minimising computer fraud. Commercial video training package, followed by talk by senior auditor from the Comptroller and Auditor General's office. Group discussion on DSW problems in this area. Half-day session.
September '84	Office Automation Techniques	Full-day workshop presented by Digital Ireland in Park House, involving extensive "hands-on" experience.
October '84	Computerised Personnel Information Systems	Attendance by some MIT group members at half-day presentation and demonstration of AnCO computerised personnel information system.
	User Managers' Role in Systems Development.	Seminar by commercial consultancy on project life cycle. Identification of stages where user management involvement is critical.
	Auditing Computer Systems	An auditor's view of a secure system. Group discussion. Half-day session.

Month	Topic Covered	Presentation Details
	Strategic Planning in General and in Relation to Information Technology	Half-day workshop on the concept of strategic planning, presented by commercial consultancy.
	Strategic Planning Issues in the Department of Social Welfare	Follow-up to previous session, emphasising the Department's current and future situation.
	Towards a Management Information System	Presentation by two MIT group members on need for management information system and outline of progress to date.
	Where Do We Go From Here?	Farewell meeting. Review of MIT group programme. Discussion of possible future courses of action.

APPENDIX I

MIT Group Evaluation Questionnaire

MIT GROUP EVALUATION QUESTIONNAIRE

On balance, how would you rate the MIT Group experiment?

Please circle the number which best represents your feelings.

Relevant	1---2---3---4---5---6---7	Not relevant
Boring	1---2---3---4---5---6---7	Interesting
Difficult for me	1---2---3---4---5---6---7	Easy for me
Learned a lot	1---2---3---4---5---6---7	Learned nothing
Stimulating	1---2---3---4---5---6---7	Unstimulating
Slow	1---2---3---4---5---6---7	Fast
Technical	1---2---3---4---5---6---7	Non-technical
Passive	1---2---3---4---5---6---7	Active
Participative	1---2---3---4---5---6---7	Non-participative
Chaotic	1---2---3---4---5---6---7	Ordered
Enjoyable	1---2---3---4---5---6---7	Unenjoyable
Intellectually undemanding	1---2---3---4---5---6---7	Intellectually demanding
Demanding time-wise	1---2---3---4---5---6---7	Undemanding time-wise
Worth the time and effort	1---2---3---4---5---6---7	Not worth the time and effort

Please place an 'X' in the box that best describes your opinion.

Participating in the MIT
group programme has:

	DISAGREE			AGREE		
	strong	moderate	slight	slight	moderate	strong

Made me more aware of my
responsibilities as a user
manager

-3	-2	-1	+1	+2	+3

Motivated me to take a
more active role

-3	-2	-1	+1	+2	+3

Made me more interested in
developments outside my own
particular area of
responsibility

-3	-2	-1	+1	+2	+3

Helped me to formulate ideas
which I otherwise might not
have had

-3	-2	-1	+1	+2	+3

Reduced the mystique
surrounding computer
technology in general

-3	-2	-1	+1	+2	+3

Please place an 'X' in the box that best describes your opinion.

Participating in the MIT group programme has:

	DISAGREE			AGREE		
	strong	moderate	slight	slight	moderate	slight
	-3	-2	-1	+1	+2	+3
Made me feel less powerless and dependent as a non-specialist manager						
Made me a more sceptical consumer of technological expertise						
Increased my knowledge and understanding of information technology in general						
Made me more confident in discussions/meetings related to technological matters						
Increased my awareness of the problems and opportunities associated with the use of technology						

Please place an 'X' in the box that best describes your opinion.

Participating in the MIT group programme has:

	DISAGREE			AGREE		
	strong	moderate	slight	slight	moderate	strong

Made me think more critically about the use of technology in my own area of responsibility

-3	-2	-1		+1	+2	+3

Made me more assertive and demanding in my dealings with technical and organisation unit staff

-3	-2	-1		+1	+2	+3

Made me more aware of the need for active user involvement in the development of computer systems

-3	-2	-1		+1	+2	+3

Increased my desire to be more involved personally in the management of computer systems

-3	-2	-1		+1	+2	+3

Given the demands on senior officers' time, it was
inevitable that all MIT group members would miss some
sessions. In general, however, attendance at meetings was
very good. How did you personally manage to participate
in the programme while still maintaining your normal work
commitments? How difficult did you find it to make time
to attend meetings? (e.g., did you find that you had to
take work home with you to a greater extent than usual?)

Why did you continue to persevere in the face of these
difficulties?

Do you think it was a good idea to hold MIT group sessions
during normal working hours?
- YES

- NO - I would have preferred evening meetings
  (5pm - 8pm)

- NO - I would have preferred Saturday morning
  meetings

- No - I would have preferred meetings which
  straddled lunchtime (12am - 3pm)

- Other preference (please specify)

What do you think are the advantages and disadvantages of
the MIT group concept of group-orientated, in-house
development, compared to conventional management training
i.e., attendance at external courses?

Advantages of MIT group approach compared to conventional
management training

Disadvantages of MIT group approach compared to
conventional management training

Are you aware of any changes in your attitudes and/or
behaviour on-the-job which you would attribute (at least
in part) to your participation in the MIT group? Can you
describe an incident at work that illustrates how you
handled something differently or thought about something
differently, compared to how you would have acted a year
ago, prior to the MIT group.

One year ago, you completed this short computer literacy test. Please do the test again, scoring your current level of understanding of the concepts listed.

For each item, please choose a number based on the following scale:

1 = Absolutely no knowledge/understanding - have never even heard the term

2 = Almost no knowledge/understanding - have heard the term, but would not be able to explain it to someone else

3 = A little knowledge/understanding - could, if pressed, make a stab at explaining it to someone else

4 = A moderate knowledge/understanding - could give a reasonably good layman's explanation to someone else

5 = A good knowledge/understanding - would feel confident if asked to explain it to someone else

Batch processing _____	Mainframes, minis and _____
	micros: their pros
	and cons
	Data carriers _____
Transaction processing _____	Database _____
	Testing, e.g., systems _____
	program, acceptance
Distributed processing _____	Fallback arrangements _____
	Control reporting _____
High-and low-level _____	Post-implementation _____
languages	maintenance
	Configuration _____

System software	_____	Applications software	_____	Daisy Wheel
Turnkey packages	_____	Hardware convergence	_____	Expert systems
Structured files	_____	Time-sharing	_____	Interactive system
On-line systems	_____	Real time systems	_____	Optical character reading
Peripherals	_____	Menu-driven language	_____	Workstation
File creation	_____	File conversion	_____	CPU
Network	_____	DIANE	_____	Shared logic

Pretend it is this time last year and that you are completing the computer literacy test for the first time. Score your knowledge of the terms listed. It is possible that, with the benefit of hindsight, you would now score yourself differently!

For each item, please choose a number based on the following scale:

1 = Absolutely no knowledge/understanding – have never even heard the term

2 = Almost no knowledge/understanding – have heard the term, but would not be able to explain it to someone else

3 = A little knowledge/understanding – could, if pressed, make a stab at explaining it to someone else

4 = A moderate knowledge/understanding – could give a reasonably good layman's explanation to someone else

5 = A good knowledge/understanding – would feel confident if asked to explain it to someone else

Batch processing _____

Transaction processing _____

Distributed processing _____

High-and low-level languages _____

Mainframes, minis and micros: their pros and cons _____

Database _____

Fallback arrangements _____

Post-implementation maintenance _____

Data carriers _____

Testing, e.g., systems program, acceptance _____

Control reporting _____

Configuration _____

Systems software	___	Applications software	___	Daisy Wheel	
Turnkey packages	___	Hardware convergence	___	Expert systems	
Structured files	___	Time-sharing	___	Interactive system	
On-line systems	___	Real time systems	___	Optical character reading	
Peripherals	___	Menu-driven language	___	Workstation	
File creation	___	File conversion	___	CPU	
Network	___	DIANE	___	Shared logic	

Do you think there is any particular advantage in having
an outside person (like myself or Mary Rose Greville)
involved with a group like the MIT group? Would it have
made any difference if the "facilitator" had been an
internal DSW trainer or a CSTC trainer?

In your opinion, did the formation of the MIT group create
an "elite" within the Department? If so, what effects -
beneficial and adverse - has this had on the organisation
as a whole?

Do you think it important that groups like the MIT group
be composed primarily of officers at the same grade level?
Would a mixed group (AP to Ass. Sec.) work just as well?

If another MIT group were to be formed in the Department,
what changes in approach/content/organisation would you
advocate so as to make the experience more relevant and
worthwhile for participants?